SPORTS TEASERS

A Book of Games and Puzzles

More than 100 quizzes covering everything from baseball to log rolling

Other paperbacks in the Random House Sports Library

Born to Hit: The George Brett Story

The Masked Marvels: Baseball's Great Catchers

Winners Under 21: America's Spectacular Young Sports Champions

SPORTS TEASERS

A Book of Games and Puzzles

by
Zander Hollander and
David Schulz

*illustrated with drawings by Marsha Cohen
and photographs*

A ZANDER HOLLANDER SPORTS BOOK

Random House  New York

 Published in the United States by Random House, Inc., New York, and simultaneously in Canada by Random House of Canada Limited, Toronto.

Even quiz makers don't have all the answers. The authors acknowledge with appreciation the contributions of Eric Compton, who does wonders with word games; Phyllis Hollander; and Frank Kelly.

Manufactured in the United States of America
1 2 3 4 5 6 7 8 9 0

Introduction

Bring your pencil and enter the wild and wonderful world of sports games, puzzles, and photo quizzes. Here's your chance to match up, unscramble, tell the truth, fill in, identify, and play games. And you don't have to be a sports freak to join the fun.

There is something here for everybody—in more than 10 sports. Best of all, if you don't know the answer, maybe your friends will. The answers in the back of the book can be as much fun as the questions.

On your mark, get set, go!

Contents

CHAPTER 1

Balls and Strikes: Baseball

Scrambled Big Leaguers

Kne Rziet is really Ken Reitz's name, scrambled up. Can you figure out the other mixed-up major-league stars below? The answers are at the end of the book.

1. Jmi Rcei (Boston Red Sox)
2. Meik Sihmctd (Philadelphia Phillies)
3. Bbo Hrrone (Atlanta Braves)
4. Cielc Coreop (Milwaukee Brewers)
5. Rehiic Zkis (Seattle Mariners)
6. Gyra Mestatwh (Philadelphia Phillies)
7. Seevt Gvraye (Los Angeles Dodgers)
8. R. J. Rdhirac (Houston Astros)
9. Gsoeo Ggsoase (New York Yankees)

Easy as Pie

This major leaguer is usually on the throwing end. Here he catches a pie in a comedy role on television. Who is he? →

3

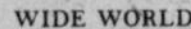
WIDE WORLD

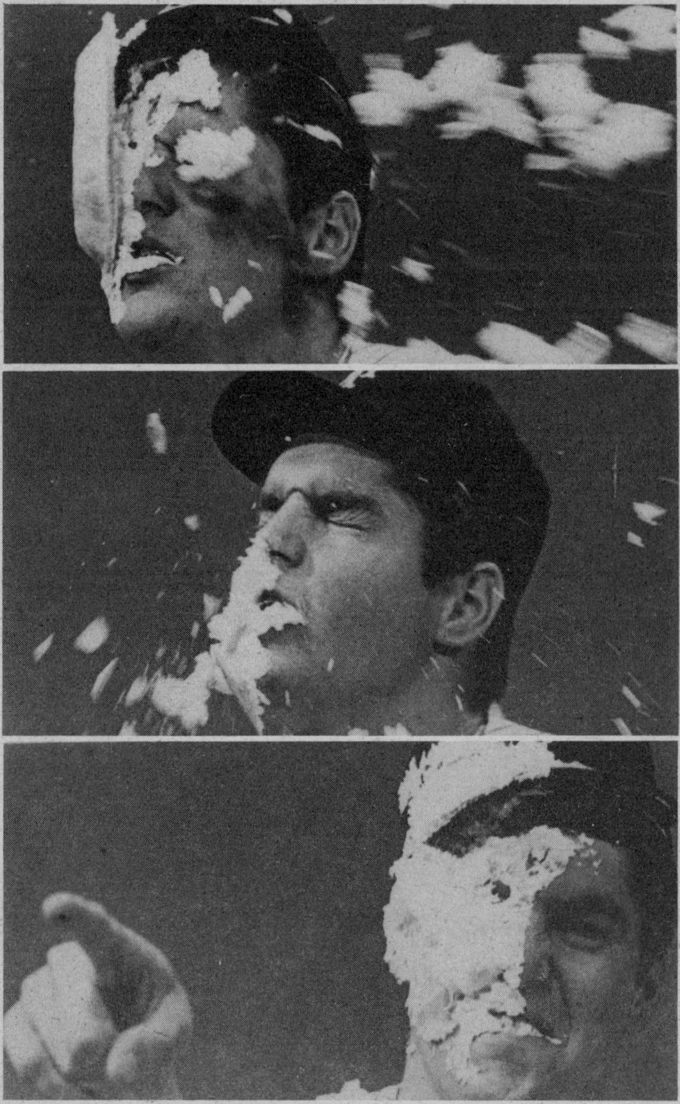

4

To Tell the Truth

1. Ralph Kiner is in the Baseball Hall of Fame. As a power hitter with the Pittsburgh Pirates in the 1940s and '50s, he led the National League in home runs seven seasons in a row, yet he was never once voted the league's Most Valuable Player. *True or false?*
2. Hank Aaron, who established a career record for home runs while playing with the Milwaukee and Atlanta Braves, never hit a home run in the American League. *True or false?*
3. In 1930 the Philadelphia Phillies' Chuck Klein batted .386 and knocked in 170 runs, but didn't lead the National League in batting or runs batted in. *True or false?*
4. Matty Alou batted over .330 three seasons in a row, yet did not win a batting title. *True or false?*
5. Although he was one of the most feared hitters of his day, batting better than .300 almost every year and collecting a lifetime total of 714 major-league home runs, Babe Ruth was never selected as the American League's Most Valuable Player. *True or false?*

6. Nobody ever stole second, third, and home in the same inning. *True or false?*
7. Forty-six rookies hit home runs in their first time at bat in the major leagues. None of them hit the first pitch on opening day for a home run. *True or false?*
8. The poem called "Casey at the Bat," which ends with the line "but there is no joy in Mudville —mighty Casey has struck out," was originally written about Casey Stengel when he was a player. *True or false?*
9. There is a baseball Hall of Famer who played in more than 150 games and who came to bat more than 650 times in one season without hitting even one home run. *True or false?*
10. A member of the losing team was never selected Most Valuable Player in the World Series. *True or false?*
11. Babe Ruth hit three home runs in his last major-league game. *True or false?*
12. Nobody who hit 40 or more home runs in a season failed to drive in at least 100 runs that year. *True or false?*
13. There was never a pitcher who, during the course of a 20-or-more victory season, pitched more winning games than he issued bases on balls. *True or false?*

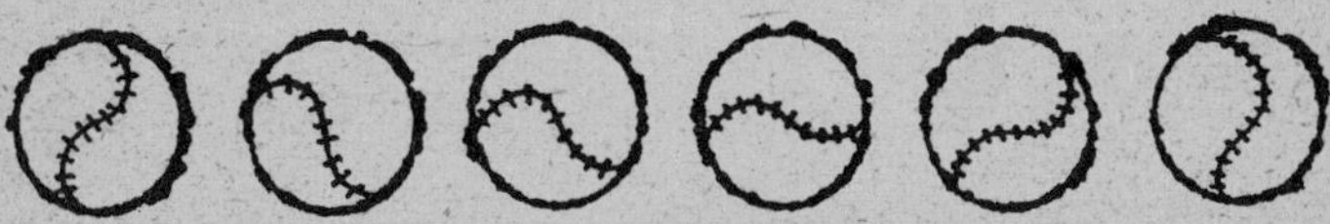

School for Thought

More and more major-league baseball players are getting their start in college. Match the players on the left with the schools they attended on the right.

1.	Richie Zisk	A.	Arizona State
2.	Dave Winfield	B.	Brigham Young
3.	Carl Yastrzemski	C.	Cal State, Fullerton
4.	Frank Tanana	D.	Indiana State
5.	Tommy John	E.	Minnesota
6.	Davey Lopes	F.	Notre Dame
7.	Graig Nettles	G.	Ohio University
8.	Mike Schmidt	H.	Seton Hall
9.	Tom Seaver	I.	San Diego State
10.	Bob Horner	J.	Southern California
11.	Dannie Ainge	K.	Vanderbilt
12.	Scott Sanderson	L.	Washburn

Good Morning, America

He was once a star first baseman at Mt. Hermon Prep in Massachusetts. Every year he gets to go to spring training with a big-league team. Who is he?

ABC-TV/SPORTS PHOTO SOURCE

8

Rain Game

You're at the ballpark and it starts to rain. The scoreboard operator, giving you something to do, flashes the puzzle below. Circle the following names among the letters: ANGEL, ASTRO, ATHLETIC, BRAVE, CARD, CUB, DODGER, EXPO, GIANT, INDIAN, JAY, MARINER, MET, ORIOLE, PADRE, PHILLIE, PIRATE, RANGER, RED, ROYAL, TIGER, TWIN, YANKEE. You can go up, down, left, right, or on a slant. Some letters will be circled more than once.

E E K N A Y O P S R I

R P T R N T D R A C O

E O H S G R E G I T X

G E G I E A S T R O M

N T E M L N E C G A D

A A T S W L U H R I D

R R G O H B I I O N O

O I E T W I N E Y D D

Y P A D R E T N A I G

E A X B R A V E L A E

R O J E L O I R O N R

Mud Pies

Lena Blackburne played 550 major-league games, mostly as an infielder between 1910 and 1929. He had a career batting average of .214. His contribution to baseball came later and it had to do with mud. What was the connection?

Home-Run Kings

Hank Aaron, Lou Gehrig, Mickey Mantle, Roger Maris, Willie Mays, Johnny Mize, Frank Robinson, and Babe Ruth were all great home-run hitters. Theirs are the only names you'll need to answer the questions below. Note that some will appear more than once.

1. Who are the only two hitters to knock 60 or more home runs in a single major-league season?
2. Who is the only switch-hitter ever to rap more than 50 homers in a season?
3. Who are the only two men to hit more than 700 home runs during their major-league careers?
4. Who is the only homer hitter to have more than 600 career homers without reaching 700?
5. Who are the only three batters to swat 50 or more home runs in a year batting left-handed?
6. Who is the only man to hit three or more home runs in a game six different times?
7. Who hit more grand-slam home runs (23) than anyone else?
8. Who is the only man to twice hit three home runs in a World Series game?
9. Who holds the career record of 16 home runs in World Series play?
10. Who is the only man to hit 20 or more homers in 20 different major-league seasons?

11. Who is the only player to hit 200 or more home runs in each major league?
12. Who holds the record for home runs hit in extra innings with 22?
13. Who hit 14 runs—the record—against Cleveland in one season?
14. Who holds the record for most home runs on the road in one season with 32?

All in the Family

Match the family name in the middle with the father who first played in the major leagues on the left, and the son who followed in his footsteps on the right.

1.	Vernon	A.	Bell	a.	Bump
2.	Maury	B.	Berra	b.	Buddy
3.	Gus	C.	Boone	c.	Dale
4.	Yogi	D.	Law	d.	Bob
5.	Ray	E.	Wills	e.	Vance

Color Guide

Which is the only current major-league baseball team that has green as one of its official colors? Which has brown?

A Comedy Team

Bud Abbott (left) and Lou Costello were comedians who did a baseball skit that has brought laughs to fans for more than 40 years. What is the name of the skit?

UPI

The Name Game

Some major-league teams have gotten special nicknames because of the way they looked or played during a winning season. Match the nickname on the left with the team on the right.

1.	Hitless Wonders	A.	1927 New York Yankees
2.	Murderers' Row	B.	1934 St. Louis Cardinals
3.	Gashouse Gang	C.	1950 Philadelphia Phillies
4.	Baby Birds	D.	1962 Chicago White Sox
5.	Mustache Gang	E.	1966 Baltimore Orioles
6.	Whiz Kids	F.	1974 Oakland Athletics

On the Platter

Match the definition in the left-hand column with the words in the right-hand column so that the menu reads correctly.

1. An easy fly ball is called a can of . . .	A. Meal ticket
2. A hard groundball may sometimes be as hard to handle as a . . .	B. Plate
3. A difference of opinion, especially between a manager and an umpire, can sometimes grow into a . . .	C. Grapefruit
4. The spring-training season in Florida is loosely organized into the . . . League	D. Corn
5. A player who makes an easy play look hard or who plays up to the fans in the stands is usually referred to as a . . .	E. Hot Potato

6.	Sometimes a pitcher delivers a ball that is ridiculously easy to hit. It looks so good that the batter might call it a . . .	F.	Rhubarb
7.	A key pitcher on a team who can usually be counted on to come through in the clutch is said to be that team's . . .	G.	Hot dog
8.	A splotchy red bruise that often appears after a base runner's hard slide is called a . . .	H.	Chop
9.	Heckling, whether from the stands or the dugout, is also called giving a player the . . .	I.	Bones
10.	A minor-league player called up by the parent team who doesn't stick around very long is said to have come up for a cup of . . .	J.	Strawberry
11.	A really skinny player is called a bag of . . .	K.	Raspberry
12.	A batted ball that bounces high into the air on the first hop is referred to as a Baltimore . . .	L.	Lollipop

13. When a batter has a very good day, it is often said that he had a feast at home . . .

M. Coffee

Between Bases

Baseball stars are not always in the limelight. Circle those who are hiding in the puzzle below: AIKENS, BRETT, CAREW, CARLTON, CARTER, DAUER, LYNN, OTT, PALMER, PUHL, RICE, ROSE, RYAN, SCHMIDT, SIMMONS, STONE, TRILLO, WALK, WILSON, WINFIELD. You can go up, down, left, right, or on a slant. Some letters will be circled more than once.

C	A	S	N	O	M	M	I	S	R	F
N	A	I	K	E	N	S	R	Y	O	W
O	C	R	R	E	T	R	A	C	I	A
S	Y	T	L	Y	N	N	B	K	W	E
L	S	R	B	T	P	W	S	L	T	I
I	F	I	R	W	O	E	R	A	D	V
W	D	L	E	I	F	N	I	W	I	I
E	A	L	T	E	E	O	C	S	M	L
R	U	O	T	S	E	T	E	T	H	G
A	E	W	O	T	T	S	O	U	C	O
C	R	R	E	M	L	A	P	N	S	T

Bursting the Bubble

Who is the Kansas City Royal behind the bubble in the Joe Garagiola/Bazooka Big League Bubble Gum Blowing Championship?

TOPPS/SPORTS PHOTO SOURCE

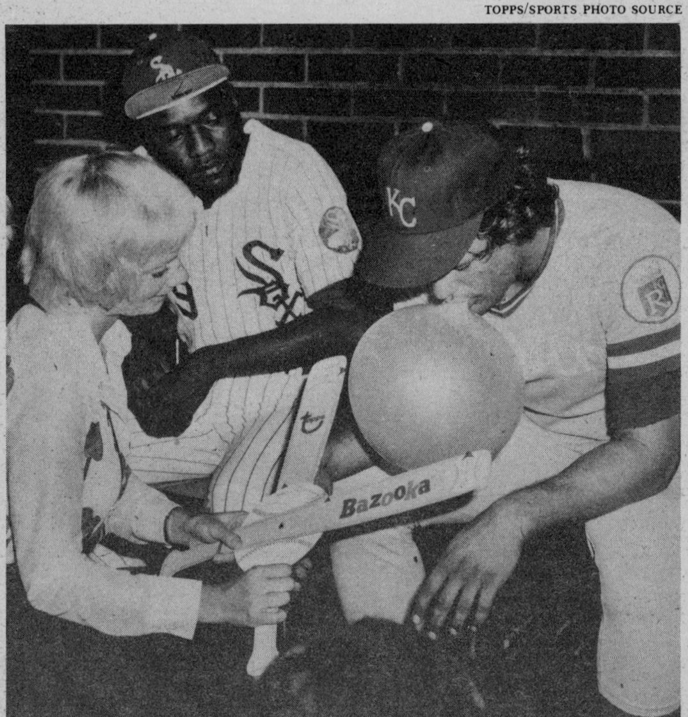

Completing the Play

Major-league baseball has been around for more than a hundred years, and many old sayings are used as much today as when they were first thought up. Fill in the missing word or words in these famous sayings.

1. A good little hitter named Wee Willie Keeler, playing in the 1890s, once explained the secret of his batting success by saying all he did was "hit 'em where they______."
   (one word)

2. A standard baseball cliché, "The game's never over until the last man is out," was reworked a few years ago by Yogi Berra when he said, "You're not out of it until ______ ____ ____ ____."
   (four words)

3. As a scout for the St. Louis Cardinals, Mike Gonzalez once sent a telegram with his report on a young prospect. All it said was, "Good field, ____ ____."
   (two words)

4. The New York Mets were created in the early 1960s and, like most new teams, they weren't the most talented bunch in the league. This prompted their manager, Casey Stengel, to ask one day, "Can't anybody here ____ ____ ____?"
(three words)

5. When Dizzy Dean played for the St. Louis Cardinals in the 1930s, he was as well known for his oddball remarks as he was for his fastball. One day, after an injury and a trip to the hospital, Dizzy told the sportswriters, "X-rays of my head showed ______."
(one word)

Unlisted Number

Ty Cobb broke many batting and base-stealing records while playing with Detroit from 1905 to 1926, yet the Tigers never retired his uniform number. Why not?

Home, Sweet Home

Match the major-league team on the left with its home field in the center, and then guess the city where the team plays on the right. (Note: Two of the cities have two different teams and stadiums.)

1. Angels	A. County Stadium	a. Anaheim
2. A's	B. Olympic Stadium	b. Arlington
3. Astros	C. Memorial Stadium	c. Atlanta
4. Blue Jays	D. Municipal Stadium	d. Baltimore
5. Braves	E. Metropolitan Stadium	e. Bloomington
6. Brewers	F. Veterans Stadium	f. Boston
7. Cardinals	G. Exhibition Stadium	g. Chicago
8. Cubs	H. Yankee Stadium	h. Cincinnati
9. Dodgers	I. Tiger Stadium	i. Cleveland

10. Expos	J. Astrodome	j. Detroit
11. Giants	K. Dodger Stadium	k. Houston
12. Indians	L. Royals Stadium	l. Kansas City
13. Mariners	M. Anaheim Stadium	m. Los Angeles
14. Mets	N. Atlanta Stadium	n. Milwaukee
15. Orioles	O. Arlington Stadium	o. Montreal
16. Padres	P. Oakland Coliseum	p. New York
17. Phillies	Q. Busch Stadium	q. Oakland
18. Pirates	R. Wrigley Field	r. Philadelphia
19. Rangers	S. Candlestick Park	s. Pittsburgh
20. Reds	T. Kingdome	t. St. Louis
21. Red Sox	U. Comiskey Park	u. San Diego
22. Royals	V. Shea Stadium	v. San Francisco
23. Tigers	W. Jack Murphy Stadium	w. Seattle
24. Twins	X. Three Rivers Stadium	x. Toronto
25. White Sox	Y. Riverfront Stadium	
26. Yankees	Z. Fenway Park	

Another Sport

What do these major-league baseball players have in common: Butch Hobson, Tom Haller, Jim Davenport, Steve Renko, and Joe Sparma?

The Rifleman

The player second from the left in the front row had a brief career in baseball's major leagues and also played for the Boston Celtics in the National Basketball Association. He later became a movie and television star. Who is he?

SPORTS PHOTO SOURCE

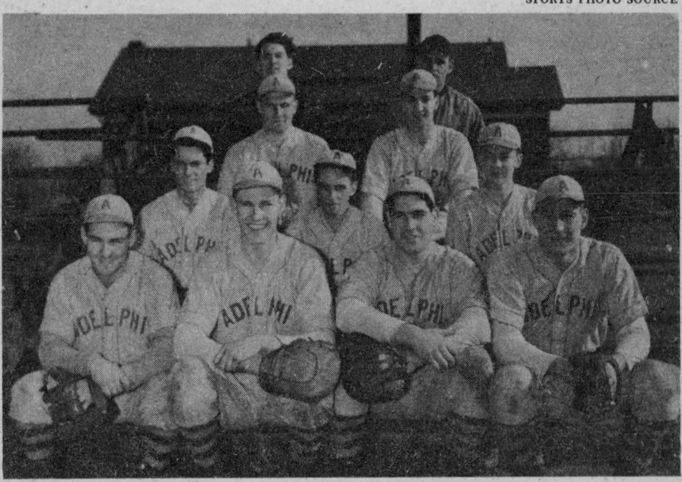

Perfection

1. In a perfect game a pitcher gives up no runs, no hits, no walks, and lets no batter reach first base, even on an error. There have been only 11 such games pitched in the history of the major leagues. The last time it was done was on May 15, 1981, by what Cleveland Indian pitcher?
2. Ernie Shore is credited with pitching a perfect game during the 1917 season, yet he wasn't even the starting pitcher in the game. How did that happen?
3. The only no-hit game ever to occur during a World Series was a perfect game hurled by Don Larsen on October 8, 1956. What two teams were involved?
4. In that perfect World Series game, Larsen's control was so good that only one batter had as many as three balls on him, and that was in the first inning. How many pitches did Larsen throw in the nine innings of the perfect game?
5. On September 9, 1965, Sandy Koufax of the Los Angeles Dodgers threw the fourth no-hitter of his career on the way to a perfect game against the Chicago Cubs. The four no-hitters were the most ever by a major-league pitcher. Yet this game also went into the record books for another reason. What was it?

Quick Change

In 1922 Max Flack of the Chicago Cubs played against Cliff Heathcote of the St. Louis Cardinals in the first game of a doubleheader. In the second game the same two men played against each other, but Flack was wearing a Cardinals' uniform and Heathcote was wearing a Cubs'. How did that happen?

Crosstown Rivalries

Several cities used to be represented by two or more major-league baseball teams, as Chicago is today with the National League Cubs and the American League White Sox. Match the cities on the left with the two (or three) major-league teams on the right that once played there at the same time.

1. New York
2. Boston
3. Philadelphia
4. Los Angeles
5. St. Louis

A. A's
B. Angels
C. Braves
D. Browns
E. Cardinals
F. Dodgers
G. Giants
H. Phillies
I. Red Sox
J. Yankees

Mound Magic

In 1906 Nick Altrock of the Chicago White Sox won a game without throwing a pitch. How did it happen?

Mystery Ms.

She could play any sport, and she was voted the Woman Athlete of the Half-Century in 1950. She won two Olympic gold medals and one silver in track and field, and was an outstanding golfer. She's shown here with the Philadelphia Athletics' Jimmie Foxx at spring training in the 1930s. Who is she, and did she ever pitch in the major leagues?

UPI

A Rare Byrd

Sammy Byrd was a professional golfer who won 23 tournaments in the late 1930s and early 1940s. But before that he was a major-league baseball player with the nickname Babe Ruth's Legs. How did he come to be called that?

An Old Oriole

Brooks Robinson, the Hall of Fame third baseman, spent his entire major-league career with the Baltimore Orioles. When he retired after the 1977 season, he had set a major-league record for years with the same team. How many was it? a. 21, b. 22, c. 23, d. 24

Triple Threat

Hitting records are some of the most familiar in baseball. One of the least remembered, however, is the most triples hit in a single season. A triple is the hardest hit for a batter to achieve, since it requires a well-hit ball between outfielders and a speedy runner to make it to third base. The most triples hit in one season were by Pittsburgh's J. Owen Wilson in 1912. What was his total, unmatched since then?

Old-Timers

Baseball is thought of as a young man's game. Yet three players who began their careers in the 1950s were still playing in the 1980s. Who are these four-decade players?

Another player who ended his career in the 1980s was the only five-decade man to play in the majors. Was it Willie Mays, Warren Spahn, Minnie Minoso, or Hoyt Wilhelm?

Peanuts, Popcorn

He played sandlot baseball as a youngster and was once on the United States Naval Academy cross-country running team. In the mid-to-late 1970s he got a chance to bat—and pitch—in slow-pitch softball. Who is he?

→

UPI

Baseball Boggling

The bases are loaded with two out in the last of the ninth, the score is tied, and you're the hitter. Here's your chance to win the game by finding these baseball terms in the puzzle below: BALL, BAT, BUNT, HIT, MITT, OUT, RUN, SAFE, SLIDE, TAG. Spell out each word, drawing a continuous line from letter to letter. You can go up, down, left, right, and on a slant—but you can't jump over any letter. Some letters will be used more than once.

B	U	T	A	G
R	N	A	F	E
O	U	S	I	D
T	L	L	M	T
B	A	H	I	T

CHAPTER 2

Kickoff: Football

Scrambled Quarterbacks

Rcrdiah Tdod can be rearranged to spell Richard Todd. Can you unscramble the names of the other NFL quarterbacks listed below?

1. Dnayn Wtieh
2. Bnira Sepi
3. Btre Jseno
4. Dna Fusot
5. Rno Jkrwoais
6. Jmi Zrno
7. Vcien Eansv
8. Jeo Tsnneimha
9. Sveet Ggnrao
10. Setev Bkkwaoitsr

Handsome Hero

He played a convict who quarterbacked his fellow prisoners in a game against the warden's team. The movie is *The Longest Yard*. Who is he? ⟶

PARAMOUNT PICTURES/SPORTS PHOTO SOURCE

Lights, Camera, Action ...

Match the National Football League stars on the left with the movies in which they appeared on the right.

1.	Fred Williamson	A.	*Caveman*
2.	Otis Sistrunk	B.	*The Towering Inferno*
3.	John Matuszak	C.	*The Longest Yard*
4.	Alex Karras	D.	*Blazing Saddles*
5.	Jim Brown	E.	*Black Caesar*
6.	Ray Nitschke	F.	*Car Wash*
7.	O. J. Simpson	G.	*The Dirty Dozen*

Alias

Fill in the blanks with the nicknames or initials by which these National Football League stars are known.

1. Christian Adolph _ _ _ _ _ Jurgensen III
2. Junius _ _ _ _ Buchanan
3. David _ _ _ _ _ _ Jones

4. Charles _______ Smith
5. Bryan _____ Starr
6. Lander ____ Bacon
7. Robert _______ Bleier
8. Charles Edward _____ ____ Greene
9. Dwight ___ Lewis
10. Billy _______ _______ Johnson
11. Elisha _________ Manning III

Wrong-Way Runs

Linemen are the unsung heroes of the game, performing their chores with little recognition while the receivers, running backs, and quarterbacks score the points and get the glory. Still, almost every football lineman dreams of that one moment in his career when he can become a hero. So when a lineman gets a chance to score, he is likely to be very excited over the opportunity.

Roy Riegels of the University of California was such a lineman. He was playing in the Rose Bowl on New Year's Day, 1929, against Georgia Tech. Early in the second quarter, with no score in the game, Tech had the ball on its own 25-yard line. Tech's Stumpy Thomason carried the ball into the line for five yards, but then fumbled. That was Riegels' chance. Scooping the ball up on a dead run, Riegels headed for the

Tech goal line, twisting and turning to avoid the would-be tacklers.

There was just one more pack of Tech men to avoid. Instead of plowing into them, Riegels made a sharp turn and, getting his direction mixed up, began heading toward his own goal line. Now it was Riegels' own California teammates who were chasing him and trying to tackle him. One of them, Benny Lom, finally hauled Riegels down before he entered the wrong end zone. But the damage was done. California had the ball on its own 1-yard line. On the very next play Tech blocked a punt for a safety. Those two points provided the margin of victory in an 8–7 triumph by Georgia Tech.

Some 35 years later a defensive lineman with the Minnesota Vikings of the NFL also scooped up a fumble and also ran the wrong way. He rambled 60 yards, only to discover that he had scored a safety for the other team. Name this wrong-way Viking.

Varsity Show

Through the years many college football heroes have earned nicknames that will live forever, whether they played in the 1920s or just yesterday. Match the nicknames on the left with the players on the right who earned them.

1. Illinois' Galloping Ghost
2. Wisconsin's Crazylegs
3. Southern California's Orange Juice
4. Ohio State's Hopalong
5. North Carolina's Choo Choo
6. Navy's Dodger
7. Army's Mr. Inside
8. Army's Mr. Outside
9. Georgia's Fireball
10. Yale's Little Boy Blue

A. Frank Sinkwich
B. Doc Blanchard
C. Charley Justice
D. O. J. Simpson
E. Red Grange
F. Albie Booth
G. Elroy Hirsch
H. Glenn Davis
I. Howard Cassady
J. Roger Staubach

In the Huddle

You can go into a huddle with your friends on this one, or you can play it yourself. Circle the following NFL players in the puzzle below: BRADSHAW, CAMPBELL, CARMICHAEL, CASPER, FOUTS, HARRIS, JONES, MINOR, PAYTON, PRUITT, RAY, RENFRO, SIPE, STABLER, TODD, WHITE. You can go up, down, left, right, or on a slant—but you can't jump over any letter. Some letters will be circled more than once.

R	S	I	R	R	A	H	O	L	C
E	E	B	R	A	D	S	H	A	W
N	E	P	T	U	O	G	M	F	I
F	S	A	S	V	E	P	I	S	L
R	E	U	D	A	B	J	N	T	N
O	N	D	A	E	C	F	O	A	O
F	O	H	L	C	O	B	R	B	T
T	J	L	E	U	N	D	A	L	Y
W	A	E	T	I	H	W	Y	E	A
E	M	S	A	T	T	I	U	R	P
L	E	A	H	C	I	M	R	A	C

Calling the Signals

The "D" stands for Dexter, an elementary school he attended in Brookline, Massachusetts. He was a smart little quarterback. And one day he became President of the United States. Who is he?

UPI

Just for Kicks

Kickers score more points than anyone else in professional football, so it is not surprising that the leading career scorers are the men who boot field goals and points after touchdown. (Jim Brown scored more touchdowns in his career than any other player—126—and he isn't even in the top 15 when it comes to total career points.) George Blanda, who began his career as a quarterback in 1949 and ended it as a kicker in 1975, scored more points than any other player. How many points did Blanda make during his 26-year career? a. 1,130, b. 2,002, c. 1,439, d. 1,349

A Catch to It

1. Only three receivers in pro football history have caught at least one pass in a hundred or more games in a row. Dan Abramowicz was the first to do it, while playing with the New Orleans Saints and the San Francisco 49ers. The other two are still active. Who are they?
2. The Pittsburgh Steelers were appearing in their first playoff game in 25 years on December 23, 1972, when Franco Harris made a catch now

known as the "immaculate reception." Why did it get that name?

3. Percy Howard was a rookie wide receiver with the Dallas Cowboys during the 1975 season. He is unique among all the receivers who have ever played in the National Football League. Why?

Quick Draw

In what league did these teams play: Los Angeles Chargers, Dallas Texans, New York Titans?

Teasers

Are the following statements true or false?

1. The Minnesota Vikings have never won a Super Bowl.
2. The Miami Dolphins have never lost a Super Bowl.
3. O. J. Simpson once rushed for over 2,000 yards in a season.
4. The New Orleans Saints have never made the playoffs.
5. No wild-card (non–first place) team has ever won the Super Bowl.

6. Terry Bradshaw led Pittsburgh into the playoffs in his rookie year.
7. The Chicago Bears have never won an NFL championship.
8. No team has won the Super Bowl more than three times.
9. Bart Starr never threw for 400 yards in one game.

Fast on His Feet

In real life the man on the left played for the Cleveland Browns and was one of the greatest running backs of all time. He became a movie star, and here he's kicking Ernest Borgnine in *The Split*. Who is he?

MGM/SPORTS PHOTO SOURCE

Undefeated, Untied, and . . .

It was the fall of 1941, just before America's entry into World War II. The newspapers were filled with reports from Europe, as well as from the East, where Japan was making increasingly aggressive moves. The sports pages offered some relief from the grim news of the world, and sports fans in New York and Philadelphia were reading of the exploits of Plainfield Teachers College and its star halfback, Johnny Chung. Plainfield was undefeated and unscored-upon, the newspapers reported, and halfback Chung kept his strength up during the game by eating rice at halftime.

Week after week readers were fascinated by the exploits of little Plainfield Teachers and its Chinese star. Although Plainfield was never defeated, it wasn't invited to any bowl games. And Johnny Chung got no recognition—not even honorable mention—on any of the post-season All-American teams for a very unusual reason. What was it?

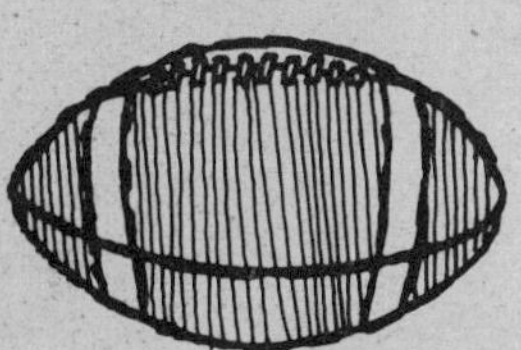

Locate the Bowl

Match the post-season college football bowl game with the city in which it is played.

1. Rose Bowl
2. Orange Bowl
3. Cotton Bowl
4. Sugar Bowl
5. Hula Bowl
6. Gator Bowl
7. Sun Bowl
8. Tangerine Bowl
9. Bluebonnet Bowl
10. Peach Bowl
11. Garden State Bowl
12. Holiday Bowl
13. Hall of Fame Bowl
14. Fiesta Bowl
15. Independence Bowl
16. Liberty Bowl

A. Atlanta, Georgia
B. Birmingham, Alabama
C. Tempe, Arizona
D. Dallas, Texas
E. East Rutherford, New Jersey
F. Shreveport, Louisiana
G. San Diego, California
H. Houston, Texas
I. New Orleans, Louisiana
J. Jacksonville, Florida
K. Honolulu, Hawaii
L. El Paso, Texas
M. Memphis, Tennessee
N. Miami, Florida
O. Orlando, Florida
P. Pasadena, California

Punt Parade

Sammy Baugh was a quarterback who played in the NFL in the 1930s and '40s and has the best punting average of any experienced kicker. His 45.1-yards-per-kick average is the all-time best. But he played in an era when punting was not as common as it is today. Jerrel Wilson, for instance, played 16 years in the AFL and NFL, through 1978. Baugh also played 16 years, but he kicked only 338 times compared to Wilson's 1,077. Since Baugh also played quarterback and defensive back, he wasn't used as a punter all the time, while Wilson was a punting specialist. Wilson is the all-time career leader in total yardage on punts. How many total yards did Wilson's kicks cover in his career? a. 28,678, b. 34,127, c. 22,833, d. 46,139

Justice Prevails

He was a football star—basketball, too—at the University of Colorado, and today he's a justice of the Supreme Court of the United States (front row, far left). Who is he?

UPI

UPI

A Tale of Suspense

Injury-riddled Alabama had its hands full in the 1954 Cotton Bowl game against the Rice Owls. Alabama's offense was in the hands of inexperienced quarterback Bart Starr, while Rice's explosive offense was triggered by halfback Dicky Moegle. Most experts had picked Rice to rout the young Crimson Tide, but Alabama stunned both Rice and the 75,504 spectators in Dallas' Cotton Bowl by taking a 6–0 lead in the first quarter.

On the first play of the second quarter, Moegle evened things up with a 79-yard touchdown run. The point after touchdown gave Rice the lead, 7–6. Alabama was not ready to collapse and battled Rice on even terms until the final seconds of the half. Rice had the ball on its own 5-yard line, and both teams lined up there for the final play. Instead of running the clock out, Rice elected to send Moegle around end with the ball. The deception worked perfectly and Moegle was soon speeding down the sideline. As he neared midfield, with the crowd urging him on, Moegle set his sights on the end zone, 95 yards from where he'd begun his run.

Moegle never made it. Why not?

Flying High

One of the problems in scheduling football games for a college team is distance. The longer the trip, the more time taken away from classes and the higher the cost of travel. In 1980 which was the most traveled team in college football?

Cumberland's Gap

Cumberland College doesn't rank among schools like Notre Dame, Alabama, Southern California, or Penn State when it comes to football heroics. Yet the tiny school in Lebanon, Tennessee, holds a big place in the record book. Why?

Galloping Backfield

The Four Horsemen of Notre Dame were so named by sportswriter Grantland Rice in 1924. They were such a force in the backfield that he called them Famine, Pestilence, Destruction, and Death. Their real names (left to right) were Don Miller, Elmer Layden, Jim Crowley, and Harry Stuhldreher. Who was their coach? a. Dan Devine, b. Gerry Faust, c. Knute Rockne, d. Ara Parseghian

UPI

On the Line

After each play in a football game, the teams are usually in a jumble. Straighten them out by circling the following NFL team nicknames: BEAR, BENGAL, BILL, BROWN, CARD, CHARGER, CHIEF, COLT, COWBOY, DOLPHIN, GIANT, JET, LION, OILER, PACKER, PATRIOT, RAM, REDSKIN, SEAHAWK, STEELER, VIKING. You can go up, down, left, right, or on a slant. Some letters will be circled more than once.

N	P	S	P	R	E	L	E	E	T	S
W	A	M	A	R	R	F	I	M	N	E
O	C	A	H	I	E	T	L	O	C	A
R	K	T	D	O	L	P	H	I	N	H
B	E	A	R	A	I	T	C	A	I	A
C	R	G	G	E	O	O	B	C	K	W
O	T	N	A	I	G	I	A	F	S	K
W	E	I	K	W	L	R	B	E	D	E
B	R	K	M	L	D	T	A	I	E	S
O	N	I	P	C	E	A	S	H	R	W
Y	C	V	S	J	O	P	T	C	C	V

Hip, Hip, Hooray

Some college football teams have earned legendary fame because of the accomplishments of special units, such as the Four Horsemen of Notre Dame. Match the wonder teams or units on the left with their schools on the right.

1.	Blocks of Granite	A.	Brown
2.	Vow Boys	B.	California
3.	Golden Avalanche	C.	Louisiana State
4.	Chinese Bandits	D.	Marquette
5.	Wonder Bears	E.	Fordham
6.	Iron Men	F.	Stanford

Game Breakers

1. When Eddie Lee Ivery was playing college football at Georgia Tech, he set a record for most yards

gained in a single game. How many yards did he gain against Air Force in 26 carries on November 11, 1978? a. 203, b. 525, c. 422, d. 356

2. Though he became a defensive back in the National Football League, Nolan Cromwell was a quarterback when he played for Kansas. As a Jayhawk, Cromwell set a rushing record for quarterbacks. How many yards did he gain in 28 carries against Oregon State on September 27, 1975? a. 294, b. 237, c. 328, d. 263
3. When Marc Wilson played quarterback for Brigham Young University, he set several passing records, including one for most yards gained in a single game. How many yards did he make completing 26 passes in 41 attempts against Utah on November 5, 1977? a. 404, b. 463, c. 571, d. 519
4. Jimmy Brown was one of the greatest running backs in the history of the NFL, retiring after the 1965 season. When he was in college at Syracuse University, Brown set a record that still stands today by scoring more points in a single game than anyone else. How many did he score on November 12, 1956, against Colgate? a. 37, b. 48, c. 39, d. 43
5. Only once in a college football game has a kicker made two field goals from a distance of 60 or more yards. Who did it? a. Russell Erxleben, Texas; b. Tony Franklin, Texas A & M; c. Matt Bahr, Penn State; d. Steve Little, Arkansas

Breaking In with a Bang

Which of these college football running backs gained 1,000 or more yards in their freshman seasons? There is more than one right answer.

a. Herschel Walker, Georgia
b. Amos Lawrence, North Carolina
c. George Rogers, South Carolina
d. Billy Sims, Oklahoma
e. Tony Dorsett, Pittsburgh
f. Darrin Nelson, Stanford
g. Vagas Ferguson, Notre Dame
h. Joe Morris, Syracuse

Surprise Ending

Two teams hoping to go to the Super Bowl were waging a classic battle the afternoon of November 17, 1968. The American Football League's defending champion Oakland Raiders were at home against the New York Jets in a game that had football fans from coast to coast glued to their television sets. With just a minute left to play in the game, the Jets were clinging to a three-point lead, 32–29, as the Raiders began to move the ball down the field. A completed pass and a 15-yard penalty brought the ball to the Jets' 43-yard line. One more good gain and the Raiders would be in field-goal range. Oakland called time out to talk things over. The fans watching on TV were treated to a commercial while waiting for the game to continue.

What happened next triggered the biggest storm of protest ever raised over an American football game.

What happened?

One for the Gipper

He played George Gipp, a Notre Dame star, in the movie *Knute Rockne—All-American*. In 1980 he took on a far more important role that had nothing to do with the movies. Who is he and what is that role?→

UPI

Football Boggling

The junior varsity team has showed up for practice. But before they can go on the field, they must find these common football terms in the puzzle below: BACK, CATCH, DOWN, END, GAIN, LOSS, PASS, RUN. Help them by spelling out each word, drawing a continuous line from letter to letter. You can go up, down, left, right, and on a slant—but you can't jump over any letter. Some letters will be used more than once.

B	K	A	T	R
A	C	C	H	U
L	O	E	N	G
P	S	D	A	I
A	S	O	W	N

CHAPTER 3

The Backboard Jumble: Basketball

Scrambled Dribblers

Aitsr Goirelm is really Artis Gilmore rearranged. Can you sort out the other mixed-up names of the NBA stars below?

1. Aavnl Aasmd (Phoenix Suns)
2. Crcdie Mlewxla (Boston Celtics)
3. Juusil Enrivg (Philadelphia 76ers)
4. Mquasre Jnnhoso (Milwaukee Bucks)
5. Snwe Nerat (San Diego Clippers)
6. Kamere Albud-Jbaabr (Los Angeles Lakers)
7. Greeog Gvnrei (San Antonio Spurs)
8. Aadirn Dleanyt (Utah Jazz)
9. Didva Tphnooms (Denver Nuggets)
10. Mhcelia Rya Rdnshicora (New York Knicks)

Bridging Leagues

Number 32 began his professional career in the American Basketball Association. In 1980–81 he was the Most Valuable Player in the National Basketball Association. Who is he? →

VIRGINIA SQUIRES/SPORTS PHOTO SOURCE

The NBA Game

Directions: Get a friend, two pieces of paper, and two pencils. Fill in the answers to the following questions. Point values are awarded for each question; at the end of each quarter total up your points. The player with the most points after the fourth quarter wins. Ready? Here's the tip-off.

First Quarter

1. The record for most points in an NBA game (173) is held by: a. Detroit, b. Cincinnati, c. Los Angeles, d. Boston. *Two points.*
2. The team that gave up those 173 points is: a. New York, b. San Antonio, c. Minneapolis, d. Denver. *Two points.*
3. The team record for most rebounds in a game is held by Philadelphia and Boston. This total is: a. between 60 and 70, b. between 70 and 80, c. between 80 and 100, d. over 100. *Three points.*
4. The record for most points in one half (97) is held by: a. Atlanta, b. Washington, c. Philadelphia, d. Los Angeles. *Two points.*
5. *True or false:* The Seattle Supersonics have never won an NBA championship. *One point.*
6. The most free throws attempted by a team in a non-overtime game is a record held by Chicago. The total is: a. between 50 and 60, b. between 60

and 70, c. between 70 and 80, d. over 80. *Two points.*

7. *True or false:* The Phoenix Suns have never won an NBA championship. *One point.*
8. The record for allowing the most points in one quarter (58) is held by: a. Denver, b. San Antonio, c. Boston, d. Indiana. *Two points.*
9. The individual record for field goals attempted in a game (63) is held by: a. Wilt Chamberlain, b. John Havlicek, c. George Gervin, d. Jerry West. *Two points.*
10. The individual record for field goals made in a game (36) is held by: a. Elgin Baylor, b. Wilt Chamberlain, c. George Gervin, d. Kareem Abdul-Jabbar. *Two points.*
11. The individual record for free throws attempted in a game (32) is held by: a. Bob Cousy, b. Rick Barry, c. Calvin Murphy, d. Wilt Chamberlain. *Two points.*
12. The individual record for free throws made in a game (28) is held by: a. Calvin Murphy, b. John Havlicek, c. Wilt Chamberlain, d. Julius Erving. *Two points.*

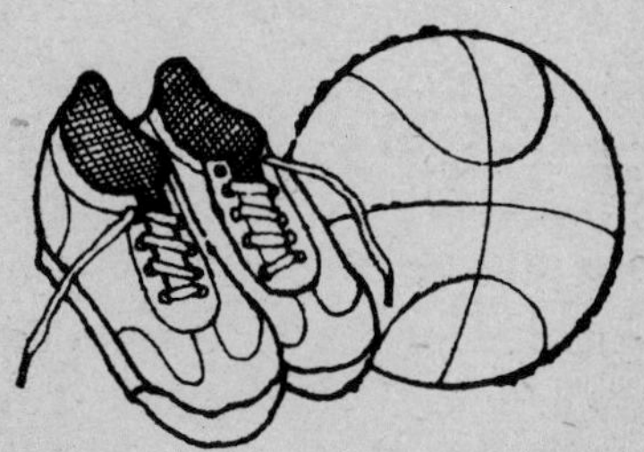

Second Quarter

Match the NBA player with his nickname. *Two points for each correct answer.*

1.	Julius Erving	A.	Sugar
2.	Wilt Chamberlain	B.	Silk
3.	George Gervin	C.	Chocolate Thunder
4.	Pete Maravich	D.	Magic
5.	Bob Love	E.	Butterbean
6.	Billy Cunningham	F.	Odie
7.	Earvin Johnson	G.	Iceman
8.	Darryl Dawkins	H.	The Kangaroo Kid
9.	Michael Ray Richardson	I.	The Stilt
		J.	Downtown
10.	Freddie Brown	K.	Dr. J
11.	Adrian Smith	L.	Pistol
12.	Jamaal Wilkes		

Three-pointer at the buzzer: Wilt Chamberlain holds the record for scoring in a game, 100 points against the Knicks on March 2, 1962. In what city did Chamberlain set his scoring record?

Third Quarter

1. The individual record for assists in a game (29) is held by: a. Kevin Porter, b. Bob Cousy, c. Nate Archibald, d. Calvin Murphy. *Two points.*
2. The individual record for assists in a season (1,099) is held by: a. Oscar Robertson, b. Nate Archibald, c. Kevin Porter, d. Bob Cousy. *Two points.*

3. The individual record for assists by a center in a season (702) is held by: a. Alvan Adams, b. Wilt Chamberlain, c. Bill Russell, d. Kareem Abdul-Jabbar. *Two points.*
4. *True or false:* There was once an NBA team in Rochester, New York. *One point.*
5. *True or false:* There was once an NBA team in Buffalo. *One point.*
6. The team record for most wins in a season (69) is held by: a. Boston, b. New York, c. Los Angeles, d. Portland. *Two points.*
7. The team record for most losses in a season (73) is held by: a. New Jersey, b. Dallas, c. Houston, d. Philadelphia. *Two points.*
8. The individual record for blocked shots in a game (17) is held by: a. Elmore Smith, b. Bill Russell, c. Wilt Chamberlain, d. Artis Gilmore. *Two points.*
9. The record for steals in a game (11) is held by: a. Dennis Johnson, b. Michael Cooper, c. Larry Bird, d. Larry Kenon. *Two points.*
10. *True or false:* There was once an NBA team in Sheboygan. *One point.*
11. *True or false:* There was once an NBA team in Miami. *One point.*
12. Wilt Chamberlain scored 70 or more points in a game: a. ten times, b. eight times, c. six times, d. three times. *Three points.*
13. The only person other than Chamberlain ever to score 30 field goals in a game is: a. Rick Barry,

b. David Thompson, c. Kareem Abdul-Jabbar, d. Elgin Baylor. *Three points.*

14. *True or false:* The Detroit Pistons have never won a championship. *One point.*
15. *True or false:* The Washington Bullets have never won a championship. *One point.*
16. *True or false:* The Philadelphia 76ers have never won a championship. *One point.*

Fourth Quarter

1. Match the team with the city in which it started in the NBA. *Two points each.*

a.	Los Angeles Lakers	A.	Philadelphia
b.	Kansas City Kings	B.	Fort Wayne
c.	Golden State Warriors	C.	San Diego
d.	Houston Rockets	D.	Minneapolis
e.	Philadelphia 76ers	E.	Buffalo
f.	Utah Jazz	F.	Syracuse
g.	San Diego Clippers	G.	Rochester
h.	Detroit Pistons	H.	New Orleans

2. The highest scorer in the history of the NBA playoffs is: a. John Havlicek, b. Jerry West, c. Bill Russell, d. Kareem Abdul-Jabbar. *Two points.*
3. *True or false:* Oscar Robertson never played on a championship team. *One point.*
4. *True or false:* Pete Maravich never played on an NBA championship team. *One point.*

5. The playoff record for points in a game (61) is held by: a. Adrian Dantley, b. Wilt Chamberlain, c. Elgin Baylor, d. Bob Cousy. *Two points.*
6. The playoff record for foul shots in a game (30) is held by: a. Wilt Chamberlain, b. Bob Cousy, c. Elgin Baylor, d. John Havlicek. *Two points.*
7. The only man to be voted Most Valuable Player of the playoffs *twice* is: a. Bill Russell, b. Kareem Abdul-Jabbar, c. Bill Walton, d. Willis Reed. *Three points.*
8. The man who holds the record for most playoff games played is: a. Paul Silas, b. John Havlicek, c. Wilt Chamberlain, d. Bill Russell. *Two points.*
9. *Last-second shots:* Match the player with the school he attended: *One point each.*

a.	Wilt Chamberlain	A.	Notre Dame
b.	Jerry West	B.	Louisiana State
c.	David Greenwood	C.	West Virginia
d.	Pete Maravich	D.	Kansas
e.	Adrian Dantley	E.	UCLA
f.	Bill Russell	F.	Michigan State
g.	Earvin Johnson	G.	San Francisco

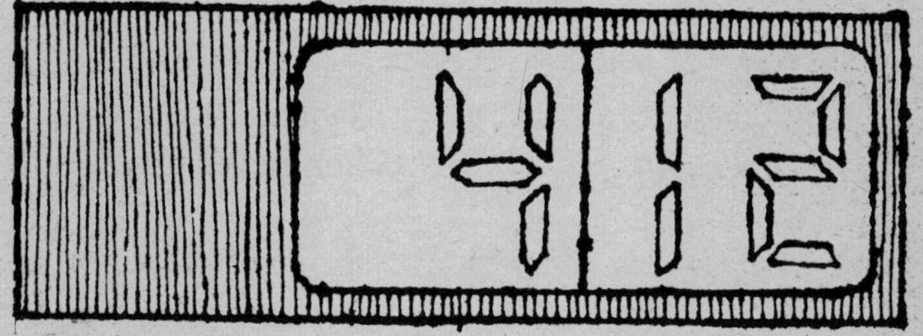

Woody Dribbles

Yes, it's Woody Allen, a big basketball fan. Which is his favorite pro team?

EILEEN MILLER

Around the Hoop

1. Which of the following players averaged 20 points and 20 rebounds during their college careers? There is more than one right answer.
   a. Bill Walton, UCLA
   b. Julius Erving, Massachusetts
   c. Walter Dukes, Seton Hall
   d. Bill Russell, San Francisco
   e. Elgin Baylor, Idaho and Seattle
   f. Adrian Dantley, Notre Dame
   g. Paul Silas, Creighton
   h. Artis Gilmore, Jacksonville
   i. Marques Johnson, UCLA
   j. Kermit Washington, American University
2. Pete Maravich is the only major college player to average more than 40 points a game during his varsity career. Performing at Louisiana State during 1968–1970, Pistol Pete scored at a clip of 44.2 points per game. Which six of these other players averaged 30 or more points during their college careers?
   a. Kareem Abdul-Jabbar (as Lew Alcindor), UCLA
   b. Larry Bird, Indiana State

c. Elvin Hayes, Houston
d. Calvin Murphy, Niagara
e. Bob McAdoo, North Carolina
f. David Thompson, North Carolina State
g. Oscar Robertson, Cincinnati
h. Rick Barry, Miami (Florida)
i. Austin Carr, Notre Dame
j. Bill Bradley, Princeton

3. Since 1960 only four players have averaged 20 or more rebounds a game during their varsity careers at a major college. Which four did it?
   a. Swen Nater, UCLA
   b. Artis Gilmore, Jacksonville
   c. Paul Silas, Creighton
   d. Elvin Hayes, Houston
   e. Kermit Washington, American University
   f. Billy Paultz, St. John's
   g. Maurice Lucas, Marquette
   h. Julius Erving, Massachusetts
4. Scoring and rebounding are two very important offensive skills. Which seven of the following players scored 2,000 points and grabbed 1,000 rebounds during their college careers?
   a. Greg Kelser, Michigan State
   b. Larry Kenon, Memphis State
   c. Billy Knight, Pittsburgh
   d. Bob Lanier, St. Bonaventure
   e. Bill Cartwright, San Francisco
   f. Michael Brooks, LaSalle
   g. Calvin Natt, Northeast Louisiana

h. Wayne Rollins, Clemson
i. Mike Gminski, Duke
j. Joe Barry Carroll, Purdue

5. In rebounding, no one has ever led the major colleges three years in a row. *True or false?*

Name Tags

Match the former NBA stars' nicknames on the left with their last names on the right.

1.	Hot Rod	A.	Fulks
2.	Jungle Jim	B.	McGuire
3.	Easy Ed	C.	Hundley
4.	Tricky Dick	D.	Macauley
5.	Jumpin' Joe	E.	Luscutoff

High-School Wonders

Since 1956 only six high-school basketball players have been named scholastic All-Americans three years in a row. Match these players on the left with the colleges they attended on the right.

1.	Earl Jones	A.	St. John's (N.Y.)
2.	Jerry Lucas	B.	Duke
3.	Wayne McKoy	C.	District of Columbia U.
4.	Lew Alcindor (Kareem Abdul-Jabbar)	D.	Maryland
5.	Albert King	E.	Ohio State
6.	Gene Banks	F.	UCLA

Pivot Play

These players usually soar high over the rim, tapping in rebounds or whipping the ball out to their teammates to start a fast break. But in this game they're lost in the crowd. Find them by circling their names in the puzzle below: BIRD, BIRDSONG, DANTLEY, DREW, ERVING, FREE, GERVIN, HIGH, ISSEL, JOHNSON, JONES, KENON, MIX, NATT, THEUS, WEDMAN, WESTPHAL, WILKES, WINTERS. You can go up, down, left, right, or on a slant—but you can't jump over any letter. Some letters will be circled more than once.

B	T	T	A	N	O	S	N	H	O	J
I	F	L	S	I	X	T	O	R	O	N
R	Y	E	T	V	E	H	N	N	E	A
D	E	S	D	R	I	B	E	F	W	W
S	L	S	V	E	C	S	K	U	E	S
O	T	I	A	G	R	W	O	S	D	E
N	N	F	R	E	E	A	T	N	M	M
G	A	S	T	R	S	P	Y	T	A	I
A	D	N	D	T	H	E	U	S	N	X
H	I	G	H	A	Y	E	S	R	F	O
W	Y	O	L	L	S	E	K	L	I	W

A Fitting Label

Even though they are no longer playing, these professional basketball stars had distinctive nicknames that live on. Match the player on the left with his nickname on the right.

1.	Oscar Robertson	A.	Mr. Clutch
2.	Wilt Chamberlain	B.	Big Red
3.	Jerry West	C.	The Big O
4.	Earl Monroe	D.	Satch
5.	Walt Frazier	E.	The Big Dipper
6.	Dave Cowens	F.	The Horse
7.	Harry Gallatin	G.	The Pearl
8.	Tom Sanders	H.	Clyde

The Other League

The American Basketball Association featured many stars who were also high scorers in the NBA after the two leagues merged in the mid-1970s, including Julius Erving, George Gervin, Moses Malone, and

Artis Gilmore. And although the Indiana Pacers, the San Antonio Spurs, the Nets, and Denver joined the NBA in the merger, several other teams were disbanded. Match the one-time ABA franchises on the left with the team nicknames on the right.

1.	Virginia	A.	Americans
2.	Oakland	B.	Amigos
3.	San Diego	C.	Buccaneers
4.	Memphis	D.	Capitals
5.	New Orleans	E.	Chaparrals
6.	Dallas	F.	Condors
7.	Houston	G.	Conquistadors
8.	Minnesota	H.	Cougars
9.	Pittsburgh	I.	Mavericks
10.	Carolina	J.	Muskies
11.	New Jersey	K.	Nets
12.	Washington	L.	Oaks
13.	New York	M.	Spirits
14.	Anaheim	N.	Squires
15.	St. Louis	O.	Tams

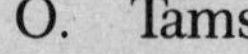

Hidden Hoopsters

Circle the following nicknames below: BUCK, BULL, BULLET, CELTIC, CLIPPER, HAWK, KING, KNICK, LAKER, MAVERICK, NET, PACER, PISTON, SPUR, SUN, SUPERSONIC, TRAILBLAZER. You can go up, down, left, right, or on a slant. Some letters will be circled more than once.

R	R	E	K	A	L	K	N	I	C	K
E	K	W	O	C	T	I	C	W	E	H
Z	S	A	G	N	I	K	L	L	U	B
A	B	U	C	K	B	R	E	C	A	P
L	T	N	N	G	R	C	E	O	S	T
B	E	H	A	W	K	L	A	V	E	R
L	L	N	O	T	S	I	P	T	A	M
I	L	R	K	E	W	P	O	A	E	M
A	U	U	U	T	A	P	W	S	I	N
R	B	O	B	P	C	E	L	T	I	C
T	C	I	N	O	S	R	E	P	U	S

A Slamdunk in Hollywood

Number 70 played basketball and football at Temple University before he became an actor and comedian. Here he's playing in an exhibition game in Los Angeles. Who is he?

UPI

Basketball Boggling

Action under the boards can often get scrambled. Players fight for loose balls, bodies collide, fouls are called. Can you find the common basketball terms that are scrambled in the puzzle below: DUNK, FOUL, GOAL, HOOK, JUMP, NET, RIM, SHOT. Spell out each word, drawing a continuous line from one letter to another. You can go up, down, left, right, and on a slant—but you can't jump over any letter. Some letters will be used more than once.

R	M	J	N	E
P	I	O	S	T
M	J	G	H	O
O	U	A	O	K
F	L	D	U	N

CHAPTER 4

Face-off: Ice Hockey

Scrambled Icemen

Dines Pivnot is really the name of National Hockey League All-Star defenseman Denis Potvin, shuffled around. What other NHL stars' names can be found in the combinations below?

1. Bboyb Ckealr (Philadelphia Flyers)
2. Lrray Roonnibs (Montreal Canadiens)
3. Mcra Tidfar (Montreal Canadiens)
4. Meki Byoss (New York Islanders)
5. Rno Dauuyg (New York Rangers)
6. Creilha Smirem (Los Angeles Kings)
7. Wneya Gzeyrtk (Edmonton Oilers)
8. Mkei Ltiu (St. Louis Blues)
9. Dyrarl Selrtit (Toronto Maple Leafs)
10. Wyaen Bcbhay (St. Louis Blues)

Leading Man

He's the star of a minor-league hockey team in the movie *Slap Shot*. Who is he? →

UNIVERSAL/SPORTS PHOTO SOURCE

Think Rink

Is that a penguin on the ice? Can someone sweep up that maple leaf? It happens every night in the National Hockey League, which has some colorful team nicknames. Circle these nicknames in the puzzle below: BLACK HAWK, BLUE, BRUIN, CANUCK, FLAME, FLYER, ISLANDER, JET, KING, MAPLE LEAF, NORTH STAR, OILER, PENGUIN, RANGER, RED WING, ROCKIE, SABRE, WHALER. You can go up, down, left, right, or on a slant. Some letters will be circled more than once.

S	N	I	U	G	N	E	P	T	E	S
K	R	F	C	C	N	T	O	U	S	E
I	E	A	I	A	O	I	L	K	A	I
N	D	E	R	N	R	B	W	O	B	K
G	N	L	E	U	T	A	S	D	R	C
O	A	E	N	C	H	I	J	E	E	O
N	L	L	A	K	S	E	G	S	B	R
I	S	P	C	O	T	N	S	O	E	S
U	I	A	E	M	A	L	F	Y	N	F
R	L	M	P	R	R	E	L	A	H	W
B	R	E	L	I	O	F	P	N	I	T

On the Line

The two wingers and a center on a hockey team are referred to as a line, and many of these combinations have earned memorable nicknames. Match the threesome on the left with their nickname on the right.

1. Clark Gillies, Mike Bossy, and Bryan Trottier
2. Bobby Bauer, Milt Schmidt, Woody Dumart
3. Sid Abel, Gordie Howe, and Ted Lindsay
4. Elmer Lach, Maurice Richard, Toe Blake
5. Marcel Dionne, Charlie Simmer, Dave Taylor
6. Joe Primeau, Charlie Conacher, Busher Jackson
7. Bobby Hull, Phil Esposito, Chico Maki
8. Vic Hadfield, Jean Ratelle, Rod Gilbert
9. Gil Perreault, Rick Martin, Rene Robert

A. Detroit's Production Line
B. Montreal's Punch Line
C. Chicago's Hem Line
D. Buffalo's French Connection
E. New York Islanders' Le Trio Grande
F. New York Rangers' Gag Line
G. Boston's Kraut Line
H. Toronto's Kid Line
I. Los Angeles' Triple Crown Line

Holiday on Ice?

No National Hockey League game has been played without at least one penalty being called and without at least one goal being scored. *True or false?*

Disappearing Act

Not all teams that join the National Hockey League stick around for a long time. In the 1970s there were teams playing that no longer exist today. Match the former franchises on the left with their nicknames on the right.

1. Cleveland	A. Scouts
2. California	B. Flames
3. Kansas City	C. Golden Seals
4. Atlanta	D. Barons

Puck Soup

There's an all-star hockey squad in this puzzle. Be the coach and line them up. First circle their names: BAKER, BOSSY, CLARKE, CRHA, GARE, GARRETT, GEOFFRION, GRETZKY, HART, KEA, LAFLEUR, LEE, LEMELIN, LEY, LIUT, NETHERY, RESCH, SAVARD, SHUTT, SIMMER, SITTLER, STASTNY, TROTTIER, ZUKE. You can go up, down, left, right, or on a slant—but you can't jump over any letter. Some letters will be circled more than once.

S	G	E	O	F	F	R	I	O	N	K
D	E	B	S	A	T	U	R	G	E	R
G	K	A	H	C	S	E	R	A	G	E
A	R	K	U	N	I	L	E	M	E	L
R	A	E	T	T	E	F	A	D	S	T
R	L	R	T	H	Y	A	H	R	T	T
E	C	O	U	Z	B	L	R	A	A	I
T	R	Z	I	U	K	O	C	V	S	S
T	R	L	L	K	E	Y	S	A	T	N
R	E	A	R	E	M	M	I	S	N	O
Y	R	E	H	T	E	N	N	T	Y	P

Another Part of the Ice

The World Hockey Association competed against the National Hockey League for several seasons in the 1970s. Then, at the start of the 1979–1980 season, the NHL absorbed four WHA teams—the Quebec Nordiques, Winnipeg Jets, Edmonton Oilers, and New England Whalers—and the WHA was no more. Match these other former WHA franchises and their nicknames.

1.	Calgary	A.	Stingers
2.	Phoenix	B.	Aeros
3.	San Diego	C.	Cowboys
4.	Indianapolis	D.	Bulls
5.	Cincinnati	E.	Roadrunners
6.	Birmingham	F.	Racers
7.	Houston	G.	Mariners

Hockey Boggling

In order to make a goal, find these common hockey terms in the puzzle below: GOAL, ICE, NET, PUCK, SAVE, SHOT, SKATE, STICK. Spell out each word, drawing a continuous line from letter to letter. You can go up, down, left, right, and on a slant—but you can't jump over any letter. Some letters will be used more than once.

S A S T I

H V E C K

O L N U C

T A K A P

G O S T E

CHAPTER 5

Of Lobs and Links: Tennis and Golf

Loving Cup

The Davis Cup is one of the most prized trophies in men's tennis. Teams from all over the world have been competing for it since 1900. During 1900–1980 the United States and Australia won it 50 times between them. Which six other countries have also won it?

a. Canada
b. Mexico
c. Britain
d. India
e. Soviet Union
f. Czechoslovakia
g. France
h. Germany
i. South Africa
j. Egypt
k. Sweden
l. Italy
m. New Zealand
n. Brazil
o. Japan

Court Jester

On the court and off, Jimmy Connors has always been one of tennis' most colorful—and winning—performers. In 1974 he came within one tournament of capturing the Grand Slam (Australian, U.S., French, and English titles). Which championship did he miss?

→

WIDE WORLD

A Mixed Volley

The Wimbledon (played in England) and U.S. Open tennis tournaments are the most publicized in the world. Test your tennis I.Q. by answering these questions about them.

1. Including singles, doubles, and mixed doubles, which woman has won the most Wimbledon titles? a. Billie Jean King, b. Chris Evert Lloyd, c. Martina Navratilova, d. Evonne Goolagong Cawley
2. Björn Borg won the Wimbledon title five years running, 1976–1980, and the only time he didn't face an American in the final was 1976. Who did Borg beat for the crown that year? a. Guillermo Vilas, Argentina; b. Tom Okker, Netherlands; c. Wojtek Fibak, Poland; d. Ilie Năstase, Romania
3. The tie-breaker was introduced into tennis in an effort to shorten matches. Previously, a player had to win by two games in order to win a set. The tie-breaker was generally adopted for use in major tournaments around 1970. Since then, the longest match was played between John Lloyd and Paul McNamee in the 1979 U.S. Open. How many games did the two play before Lloyd won?

4. Since World War II only two tennis players under the age of 21 have won the U.S. men's national singles title. The first was Richard (Pancho) Gonzalez in 1948. The other was a. Jimmy Connors, b. John McEnroe, c. Guillermo Vilas, d. Arthur Ashe

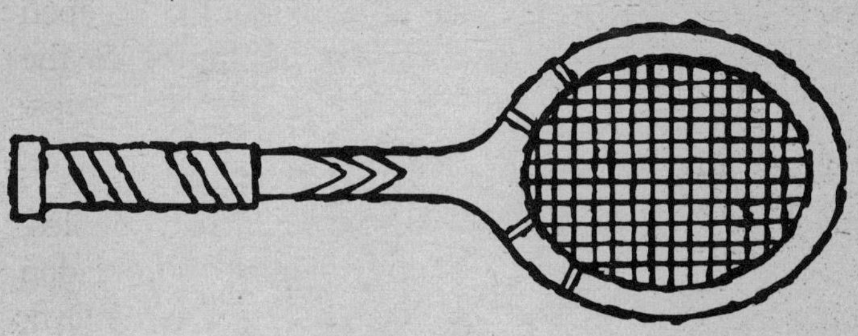

Have Racket, Will Travel

Tennis is an international sport, and most players spend more time playing in other countries than at home. On the next page, match the players on the left with their native countries on the right.

1.	Martina Navratilova	A.	Argentina
2.	Björn Borg	B.	Australia
3.	Ilie Năstase	C.	United States
4.	Andrea Jaeger	D.	Sweden
5.	Raul Ramirez	E.	France
6.	Guillermo Vilas	F.	West Germany
7.	Wojtek Fibak	G.	Hungary
8.	Betty Stöve	H.	Romania
9.	Sylvia Hanika	I.	Czechoslovakia
10.	Peter McNamara	J.	Mexico
11.	Balazs Taroczy	K.	India
12.	Gilles Moreton	L.	Netherlands
13.	Vijay Amritraj	M.	Poland

Battle of the Sexes

Men and women don't have the opportunity to compete against each other very often in most sports. But tennis is an exception, since many tournaments offer mixed doubles competition with men and women playing on the same team. In tennis singles, though, it's the usual story—with men in one tournament and women in another.

Back in 1973, for one day, it was different. There was a match between a man and a woman that not only attracted the largest in-person crowd ever to watch a tennis match, but also lured a huge national television audience. The match pitted 55-year-old Bobby Riggs against a female tennis star. Riggs had won the U.S. national championship twice and the singles title at Wimbledon before his female opponent was born. Name the famous women's champion who beat Bobby Riggs that day.

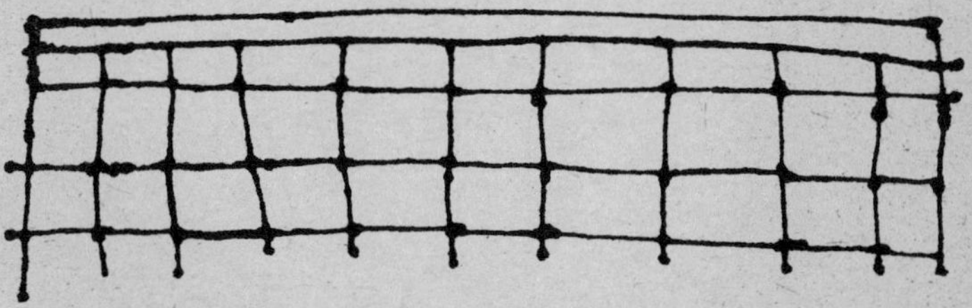

Chip Shots

1. The Masters Tournament, played each year in Augusta, Georgia, is considered the most famous golf event of all. A great golfer of the 1950s was Dr. Cary Middlecoff, a dentist who switched careers to play golf. In the 1955 Masters, Middlecoff sank the longest putt ever measured in a major tournament. How long was it? a. 51 feet, b. 64 feet, c. 72 feet, d. 86 feet
2. The record for the most holes-in-one by a Professional Golfers' Association golfer during his career is held by Art Wall, Jr. How many did he have? a. 41, b. 25, c. 56, d. 34
3. On most golf courses, par is somewhere in the low 70s, varying from course to course. Professionals regularly break par, but none had broken it in a major tournament by as much as Johnny Miller did in the final round of the U.S. Open in 1973. What was Miller's 18-hole total for that day? a. 52, b. 75, c. 81, d. 63

Prize Money

1. Professional golfers play for prize money, so it is only natural that lists are published to show which golfers won the most money. In 1980, for the first time, a woman earned more than $200,000 on the Ladies Professional Golfers' Association (LPGA) tour. Who was it? a. Beth Daniel, b. Nancy Lopez Melton, c. Sandra Haynie, d. Jane Blalock
2. Sam Snead, whose career spanned five decades, won 84 tournaments during that time. What were his career earnings? a. $1,700,000, b. $2,100,000, c. $615,000, d. $1,100,000
3. Who has won more money on the men's professional tour than anyone else? a. Arnold Palmer, b. Johnny Miller, c. Tom Watson, d. Jack Nicklaus
4. Which man was the youngest to win $1,000,000 on the pro tour? a. Johnny Miller, b. Jack Nicklaus, c. Tom Watson, d. Hale Irwin
5. In 1981 she became the first woman golfer to earn $1,000,000 during her career. Who was she?

Iron Arm

Professional golfers regularly record scores in the 70s, and the average amateur is happy when he finishes a round of 18 holes with a score of less than 100. But that's doing it with clubs. A man named Joe Flynn, says the *Guinness Book of Sports Records*, threw a golf ball around the 18-hole Port Royal course in Bermuda on March 27, 1975, setting a world record for that sort of thing. How many throws did it take Flynn to complete the 6,100-yard course?

CHAPTER 6

In the Ring: Boxing

A Comic Twist

A boxer who fought under the name of Packy East is the only man to have traded punches with Jack Dempsey, Joe Louis, Rocky Marciano, Sugar Ray Robinson, Joe Frazier, George Foreman, Muhammad Ali, and Sugar Ray Leonard. By what name is Packy East better known?

Film Fighters

Which boxers were the subjects of which movies?

1. *Rocky*
2. *Somebody Up There Likes Me*
3. *Raging Bull*
4. *The Great White Hope*
5. *Gentleman Jim*
6. *The Great John L.*

A. Jake LaMotta
B. John L. Sullivan
C. James Corbett
D. Rocky Balboa
E. Rocky Graziano
F. Jack Johnson

Ring King

Joe Louis is considered by many to be the greatest heavyweight boxing champion of all time. Certainly he was one of the most popular, both while he was number 1 (1937–1949) and up until the time he died on April 12, 1981.

1. Joe Louis earned the heavyweight crown on June 22, 1937, by knocking out James J. Braddock in eight rounds. Louis retired undefeated as champion nearly 12 years later on March 1, 1949. How many times did he successfully defend his title during that span?
2. On June 22, 1938, in the first boxing match where fans paid a total of more than $1,000,000 to attend, Joe Louis met challenger Max Schmeling of Germany. Schmeling had beaten Louis two years earlier, before Joe had become champion. Louis knocked Schmeling out in the fastest time a champion ever disposed of a challenger. How fast was the knockout?
3. One of the toughest title defenses of Louis' career came on the night of June 18, 1941, against Billy Conn, a lighter, faster fighter who was the reigning light-heavyweight champion. Conn moved up into the heavier division to meet Louis. Many experts thought Conn would be too quick and

speedy for Louis. But the champ predicted before the fight, "He can run, but he ____ ____."
(two words)

4. Born Joseph Louis Barrow on May 13, 1914, in Lexington, Alabama, Louis picked up a nickname early in his career. He was called the Brown ______.
(one word)

5. Louis reigned as champion during a time when $100,000 was considered big money for a prize-fight purse. National television coverage and closed-circuit theater showings were only distant dreams. Most of the money fighters won was paid by the people who came to see the fight in person, plus a little bit from radio stations who broadcast the event. All the fights Louis was in as champion made a total of $4,600,000. How much of this was his share? a. $2,300,000, b. $460,000, c. $1,150,000, d. $800,000

6. After an amateur career in which he was the national Amateur Athletic Union light-heavyweight champion and scored 43 knockout victories in 54 fights, Louis turned professional, patriotically enough, on July 4, 1934. He knocked out Jack Kracken in one round. How many knock-outs did Louis score in his professional career, in which he won 68 fights and lost 3?

Boxing Hopeful

Packy East (right) has the big gloves on against a former world heavyweight champion. Name the champion.

UPI

Sultan of Swat

He was one of the hardest hitters of all time, but not in boxing. Who was he?

UPI

Sweet Champion

Jake LaMotta, Randy Turpin, Carl (Bobo) Olson, Gene Fullmer, and Carmen Basilio all wore world championship belts at one time before losing them to the same man. Who is he?

Punching Bag

A good fighter must be able to take a punch, but how many knockdowns he can take is another question. On December 26, 1902, a fighter named Christy Williams set what is probably the record for the most knockdowns in one fight. It was a 17-round match against Battling Nelson. How many times did Williams go down? a. 11, b. 28, c. 35, d. 42

Clean Slate

Rocky Marciano was boxing's last undefeated world heavyweight champion. When he retired in 1956, how many fights had he won in his professional career? a. 28, b. 49, c. 54, d. 63

CHAPTER 7

The Olympic Game

Feats of Gold

Jesse Owens put on an amazing performance during the 1936 Olympic Games in Berlin, capturing four gold medals in track and field competition. In which events did he win gold?

a. 100-meter dash
b. 200-meter dash
c. 400 meters
d. 800 meters
e. 1,500 meters
f. 5,000 meters
g. 10,000 meters
h. marathon
i. 200-meter low hurdles
j. steeplechase
k. long jump
l. 100-meter relay
m. 400-meter relay

Unparalleled

Who was the first “perfect 10” in Olympic gymnastic competition?

⟶

UPI

Doubles

Match the women on the left with the Olympic events on the right in which they won two or more gold medals.

1.	Pat McCormick	A.	Swimming
2.	Wilma Rudolph	B.	Speed skating
3.	Debbie Meyer	C.	Skiing
4.	Olga Korbut	D.	Diving
5.	Sheila Young	E.	Gymnastics
6.	Andrea Mead Lawrence	F.	Track and field

Leaps and Bounds

It was during the 1968 Olympic Games in Mexico City that Bob Beamon made a long jump of 29 feet, 2½ inches that still holds as a world record. By how much did he break the old record? a. 6 ¾ inches; b. 1 foot, 9 ¾ inches; c. 2 feet, ½ inch; d. 11 ¼ inches

Roll Out the Barrel

Barrel jumping is an Olympic sport. *True or false*?

GROSSINGERS/SPORTS PHOTO SOURCE

Olympic Carnival

1. Which country has won more gold medals in the Winter Olympics than any other? a. Austria, b. Norway, c. Soviet Union, d. United States
2. What two events make up the biathlon in the Winter Olympic Games? a. cross-country skiing, b. speed skating, c. downhill skiing, d. shooting, e. cross-country running
3. The U.S. had never won an Olympic gold medal in hockey until the stunning upset at Lake Placid in 1980. *True or false*?
4. Which of the following terms are used in figure skating? a. axel, b. flush, c. icing, d. salchow, e. lutz, f. pasgang

Icy Victory

They raised the flag after the U.S. won the gold medal in hockey at the 1980 Winter Olympics. Which team did the U.S. defeat in the final game? a. Russia, b. Finland, c. Sweden, d. Czechoslovakia

WIDE WORLD

On the Button

Dick Button created *The Superstars,* a long-running television sports show. He himself was once a superstar. As a Harvard student, Button held five different major championships at one time. In what sport did he win the Olympic, World, European, North American, and United States titles?

A Winning Figure

As a 15-year-old, she won the first of her three Olympic gold medals in St. Moritz, Switzerland, in 1928. She went on to become a movie star. Who is she? a. Carol Heiss, b. Peggy Fleming, c. Sonja Henie, d. Dorothy Hamill

→

UPI

Fadeouts

Track and field, swimming, and basketball are usually the events that take over the headlines during the Summer Olympic Games. But there are many other sports in the Olympics. Since the modern Games began in 1896, a number of sports have been added and a number dropped. Which of the following sports were once on the program?

a. baseball
b. rugby
c. tug-of-war
d. tennis
e. golf
f. kung fu
g. Indian-club swinging
h. rope climbing
i. motorcycle racing
j. mountain climbing

CHAPTER 8

On Horseback

Winning the West

It was one of the last events that made the Wild West wild—a 1,000-mile horse race that started in Chadron, Nebraska, and ended up in Chicago where Buffalo Bill Cody was performing during the World's Fair. The year was 1893, and a handful of riders began the race on June 17. Each rider was allowed to use two horses and a 35-pound saddle. The combined weight of rider and saddle had to be at least 150 pounds. There was no official route, but there were 12 checkpoints along the way. How long did the winner take to finish the race?

Royal Rider

In the summer of 1981 this horseback rider made newspaper headlines and TV screens around the world, but not as a horseman. Who is he? →

WIDE WORLD

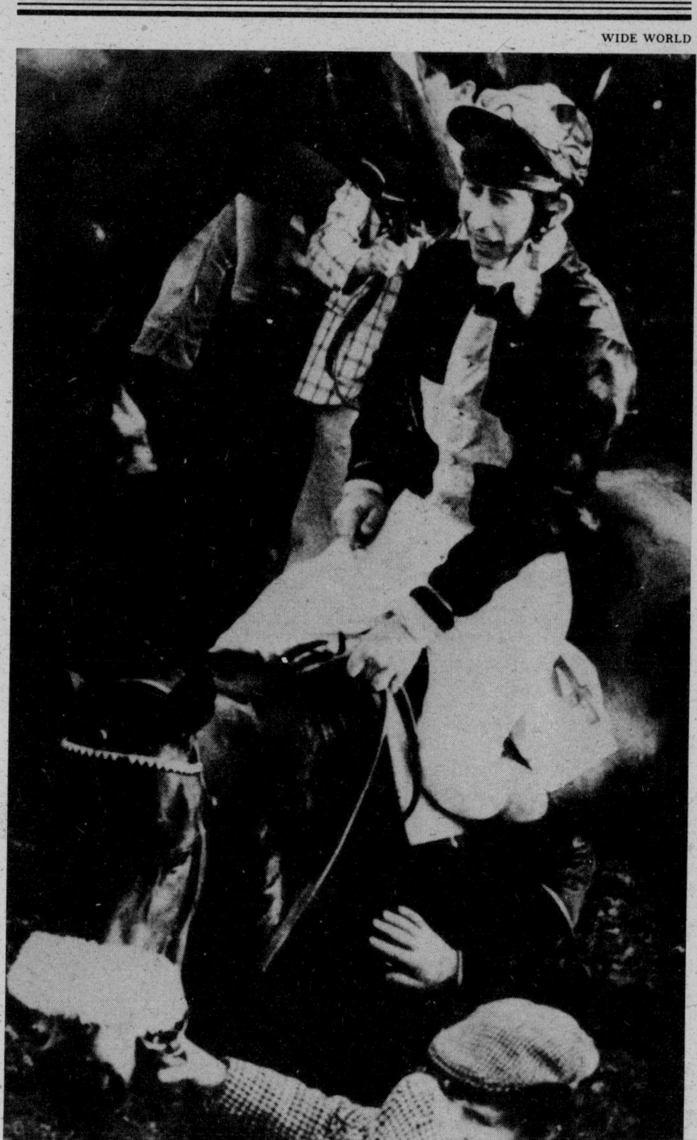

On the Right Track

Match the race on the left with the racetrack where it is held on the right.

1. Kentucky Derby
2. Preakness
3. Washington (D.C.) International
4. Flamingo
5. Louisiana Derby
6. Travers

A. Laurel
B. Saratoga
C. Churchill Downs
D. Fair Grounds
E. Pimlico
F. Hialeah

Of Phillies and Fillies

The first time the Philadelphia Phillies won a World Series game was in 1915, which was the first time a filly (a young female horse) won the Kentucky Derby. Her name was Regret. The only other time the Philadelphia Phillies won a World Series game was in 1980, which was also only the second time a filly won the Kentucky Derby. *True or false*?

The Lady in Silks

The slightly muddy woman is a jockey, the first ever to ride in a Kentucky Derby. Who is she? a. Robyn Smith, b. Princess Anne, c. Diane Crump, d. Karen Rogers

UPI

Run for the Roses

The Kentucky Derby, a race often called the Run for the Roses, is thoroughbred horse racing's biggest event. Held every year on the first Saturday in May at Churchill Downs in Louisville, Kentucky, the Derby attracts more than 100,000 fans, with millions more following the action on television and radio.

In the 1957 Derby, jockey Willie Shoemaker was aboard Gallant Man, who started off slowly in the mile-and-a-quarter race. By the time the horses were coming into the homestretch, a horse named Iron Liege had taken over the lead, with Gallant Man gaining rapidly on the outside. The two horses battled through the stretch, with Gallant Man gaining ground with every stride. As they passed the grandstand Shoemaker relaxed and stood up in the saddle, the way jockeys do when a race is over. But Gallant Man didn't win. Why?

CHAPTER 9

A Mixed Bag

Brains + Brawn

A Rhodes scholarship is one of the highest honors an American college athlete can receive, providing for two years of postgraduate study at Oxford or Cambridge universities in England. The winner is chosen for excellent grades, fondness for and success in sports, character, and leadership abilities. Match the Rhodes Scholars on the left with the sport in which they excelled on the right.

1. Senator Bill Bradley
2. TV newsman Howard K. Smith
3. Supreme Court Justice Byron White
4. Business executive Ham Richardson
5. Dr. John Misha Petkevich

A. Tennis
B. Football
C. Figure skating
D. Basketball
E. Track

Vaulting to the Moon

He was the second man to walk on the moon. He was once a center on his Montclair, New Jersey, high-school football team. And he was a pole vaulter at West Point. Who is he?

NASA/SPORTS PHOTO SOURCE

A Striking Game

1. A perfect game in bowling means throwing 12 strikes in a row. The record for the most perfect games in a career is held by Elvin Mesger of Sullivan, Missouri. How many did he bowl?
2. On March 4, 1976, John Pezzin of Toledo, Ohio, set a record for the most strikes in a row in an American Bowling Congress competition. How many was it?
3. The American Bowling Congress approves most of the bowling-league play in the United States. One of the more unusual records on its books is the most gutter balls in a row, set by Richard Caplett of Danielson, Connecticut, on September 7, 1971. How many gutter balls did he throw?

Solo Sailor

Sir Francis Chichester, at the age of 65, sailed around the world alone in his 55-foot *Gypsy Moth IV*. It took him more than a year for a round trip that began in England. How many miles did he sail? a. 23,000, b. 25,500, c. 28,200, d. 29,630, e. 32,000

Kicking It Around

Only in the North American Soccer League could you find nicknames that mean: a heavy snowstorm, a natural disaster, what a bee does. Circle the following nicknames in the puzzle below: AZTEC, BLIZZARD, BOOMER, CHIEF, COSMO, DIPLOMAT, DRILLER, EARTHQUAKE, ROUGHNECK, ROWDIE, SOUNDER, STING, STRIKER, SURF, TEA MEN, WHITECAP. Go up, down, left, right, or on a slant. Some letters will be circled more than once.

E K A U Q H T R A E K

R D I P L O M A T B C

E P A C E T I H W L E

M R W O E R G S M I N

O E D A C E T Z A Z H

O T M O H L Z B W Z G

B E S T I L R G S A U

N M T M E I D W O R O

O C I S F R U S O D R

I O N R E D N U O S S

S S G S T R I K E R T

A Battering Ram

Before he turned to acting in *Little House on the Prairie,* he was a fearless defensive lineman in the National Football League. Who is he?

NBC-TV/SPORTS PHOTO SOURCE

By the Numbers

The jersey numbers of former star players are not forgotten. Match the numbers on the left with the players on the right.

1.	Basketball's number 13	A.	Red Grange
2.	Basketball's number 44	B.	Bob Gibson
3.	Basketball's number 99	C.	George Mikan
4.	Football's number 00	D.	Wilt Chamberlain
5.	Football's number 32	E.	Hank Aaron
6.	Hockey's number 4	F.	Jerry West
7.	Hockey's number 77	G.	Bobby Orr
8.	Hall of Fame pitcher number 45	H.	Jim Otto
9.	Baseball's number 44	I.	Phil Esposito
10.	Football's number 77	J.	Jim Brown

Marathon Swim

Diana Nyad is a long-distance swimmer. One of her more unusual accomplishments was swimming around the island of Manhattan, the heart of New York City. The distance is about 28 miles. How long did it take her?

Home on the Range

As a star of radio, television, and movies, he was known as the Singing Cowboy. In baseball he is the owner of the California Angels. Who is he?

CALIFORNIA ANGELS/SPORTS PHOTO SOURCE

Streaking

1. Three major-league baseball teams shared the record of winning 10 straight games at the start of a season until the Oakland A's established a new standard in 1981. How many games in a row did the A's win at the start of that season? a. 11, b. 12, c. 13, d. 14
2. In 1931 the Philadelphia Athletics won 17 straight games during the course of the American League season. That was a league record, but it didn't come near the National League streak of the 1916 New York Giants. How many games in a row did the Giants win that year? a. 24, b. 34, c. 22, d. 26
3. The longest string of straight victories in major-college football belongs to the Oklahoma Sooners, who were unbeaten and untied in how many straight games? a. 25, b. 47, c. 33, d. 39
4. The longest winning streak in tennis history belongs to Chris Evert Lloyd, who went from August 12, 1973, until May 12, 1979, without being beaten on a clay court surface. In the semifinals of the 1979 Italian Open, Tracy Austin snapped Chris's string. How many matches did Chris win during her six-year streak? a. 60, b. 90, c. 125, d. 84
5. The first time the Los Angeles Lakers won the

National Basketball Association championship was in 1972, with Jerry West and Wilt Chamberlain leading the team. During the course of the regular season, the Lakers were unbeaten between November 5, 1971, and January 7, 1972. How many games did they win during that span? a. 33, b. 21, c. 28, d. 39

Sporting Couples

Match these athletes who became wife and husband.

1.	Olga Fikotova (discus)	A.	Ralph Kiner (baseball)
2.	Nancy Chaffee (tennis)	B.	Donald Brinker (modern pentathlon)
3.	Maureen Connolly (tennis)	C.	Jackie Jensen (baseball)
4.	Zoe Ann Olson (diving)	D.	Terry Bradshaw (football)
5.	JoJo Starbuck (figure skating)	E.	Harold Connolly (hammer throw)

Family Sports

These family members were stars in different sports. Match each athlete with his or her sport.

1. Kyle Rote, Sr.
2. Kyle Rote, Jr.
3. Billie Jean Moffitt King
4. Randy Moffitt
5. Sheila Young
6. Roger Young

A. Soccer
B. Baseball
C. Speed skating
D. Football
E. Cycling
F. Tennis

The Most Popular Run

In America athletes compete in such standard events as the 60-yard dash, the 440-yard run, and the 1-mile race. But what measured distance, not in the sport of track and field, is most frequently run in this country?

Medical Report

1. Although official statistics are not kept on broken bones and injuries, one of professional basketball's all-time leading scorers, Jerry West, probably holds the record for having one part of his body broken the most times (at least seven) during his career. What part is it?
2. David Ryder walked from Los Angeles to New York in 1970. The trip took him four and a half months. What made the feat even more remarkable?
3. Pete Gray was another athlete with a physical handicap, but he still made it to baseball's big leagues. He played the outfield and batted .218 for the old St. Louis Browns in 1945 despite what handicap?
4. Mordecai Peter Centennial Brown was a pretty good major-league pitcher, winning 238 and losing only 126 between 1903 and 1916 despite the fact that he was handicapped. Brown was missing some digits on his hand, which gave him a unique nickname. What was it?

Name Change

Match the North American Soccer League teams on the left with their former nicknames on the right.

1. Washington Diplomats
2. Montreal Manic
3. Jacksonville Tea Men
4. Calgary Boomers

A. Memphis Rogues
B. Detroit Express
C. Philadelphia Fury
D. New England Tea Men

A Touch of Sport

Which three of these famous people were once sportswriters or sportscasters?

a. Colonel Harland Sanders
b. President Ronald Reagan
c. Captain Jacques Cousteau
d. Bat Masterson
e. Pope John Paul II
f. Reverend Billy Graham
g. Ernest Hemingway

Of Skates and Scalpels

This former athlete is not playing a role in *General Hospital* or any other television program. She's a Boston surgeon who won an Olympic gold medal in figure skating in 1956. Who is she?

SUZANNE SZASZ/SPORTS PHOTO SOURCE

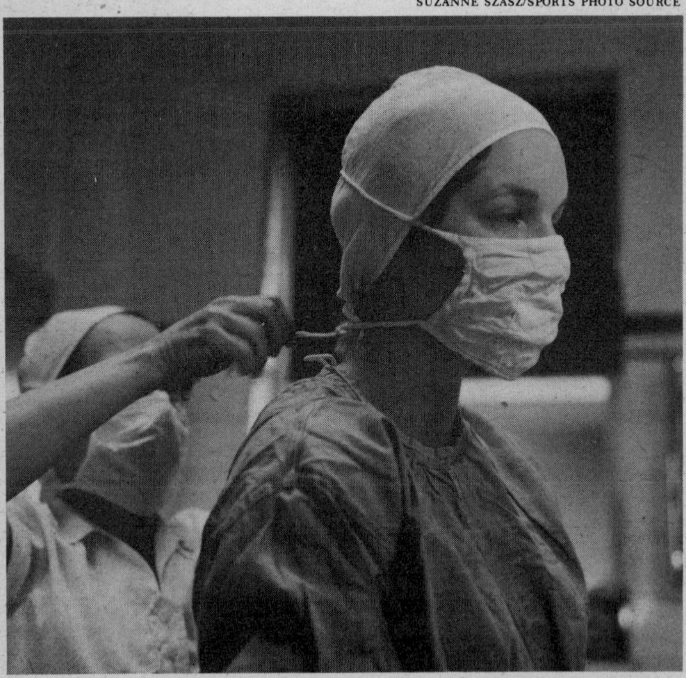

The Flush of Youth

1. Romania's Nadia Comaneci was only 14 years old when she won a gold medal for gymnastics at the 1976 Olympic Games in Montreal, yet she was not the youngest woman ever to win a gold medal. That honor belongs to Marjorie Gestring of the United States, who won the springboard diving competition in Berlin in 1936. How old was she?
2. During World War II many of the major-league baseball stars were serving overseas in the armed forces. The big-league teams were hard-pressed to find players. On June 10, 1944, the Cincinnati Reds called on hometown boy Joe Nuxhall to pitch for them. Joe did, and became the youngest player ever to reach the major leagues. How old was he?
3. The youngest player to hit a home run in the major leagues was Tommy Brown of the Dodgers on August 20, 1945, at Ebbets Field in Brooklyn. How old was he?
4. In recent years much has been made of the success of tennis teenagers like Tracy Austin, Andrea Jaeger, and Pam Shriver. Yet in 1887 teenager Charlotte (Lottie) Dod won the Wimble-

don women's singles championship, becoming the youngest champion—a distinction she still holds. How old was she?

5. In 1963 the Houston Colt .45s, as the Astros were known then, brought up an 18-year-old minor leaguer for one game at the end of the season. In his one-game appearance, John Paciorek had three hits and two walks in five trips to the plate, drove in three runs, and scored four himself. Paciorek never played another game in the major leagues. Why not?
6. Youth was also triumphant in 1958 when Jay Foster won the national table tennis championship on the Caribbean island of Jamaica. How old was he?

Brotherly Love

The odds are against any one player making it to the big leagues—in any sport. Yet there have been brothers who have made it to the top and even played together on the same team. Match the brothers on the left with their teams on the right.

1. Tom and Dick Van Arsdale
2. Johnny and Eddie O'Brien
3. Bobby and Dennis Hull
4. Jim and Gaylord Perry
5. Alex and Ted Karras
6. Billy and Tony Conigliaro
7. Al and Dick McGuire
8. George and Ken Brett
9. Pete and Frank Mahovlich
10. Mark and Marty Howe

A. Detroit Lions
B. Kansas City Royals
C. Boston Red Sox
D. Phoenix Suns
E. Montreal Canadiens
F. New York Knicks
G. Pittsburgh Pirates
H. Cleveland Indians
I. Hartford Whalers
J. Chicago Black Hawks

Fast on the Trigger

The man with the gun had a bit role in *Mission: Impossible*. He is a major-league baseball player. Who is he?

UPI

The Movie Game

Match the athletes on the left with the movies that were made about them on the right.

1. Lou Gehrig
2. Rocky Graziano
3. Jimmy Piersall
4. Glenn Davis, Doc Blanchard
5. Barney Ross
6. Dizzy Dean
7. Jack Johnson
8. Ben Hogan
9. Roy Campanella
10. Harlem Globetrotters
11. Vince Lombardi
12. Elroy Hirsch

A. *Pride of West Point*
B. *Run to Daylight*
C. *Pride of the Yankees*
D. *Fear Strikes Out*
E. *The Pride of St. Louis*
F. *Somebody Up There Likes Me*
G. *Monkey on My Back*
H. *Crazylegs*
I. *Follow the Sun*
J. *The Great White Hope*
K. *It's Great to Be Alive*
L. *Go, Man, Go*

Going Up

One of the more unusual running events each year is the Empire State Building Run-Up, a race from the ground floor to the eighty-sixth-floor observation deck of what was once the tallest building in the world. The record—set by Pete Squires, a Yonkers, New York, schoolteacher—is 10 minutes, 59 seconds. How many steps did he have to climb on his way to the deck?

Speaking of Sports

Match the sportscasters on the left with the teams they once played for.

1.	Frank Gifford	A.	Los Angeles Dodgers
2.	Tom Brookshier	B.	San Francisco 49ers
3.	Bill Russell	C.	New York Giants
4.	Don Drysdale	D.	Minnesota Vikings
5.	Don Meredith	E.	Milwaukee Braves
6.	Bob Uecker	F.	Philadelphia Eagles
7.	John Brodie	G.	St. Louis Cardinals
8.	Fran Tarkenton	H.	Boston Celtics
9.	Joe Garagiola	I.	Dallas Cowboys

Presidents in Sport

From George Washington to Ronald Reagan, the President of the United States has always recognized the importance of sport in a nation's life. Each in his own way has set an example—whether hunting and fishing, or playing baseball, football, or golf. Match these Presidents with their favorite sports.

1.	Franklin Roosevelt	A.	Fox hunting
2.	Dwight Eisenhower	B.	Wrestling
3.	George Washington	C.	Softball, jogging
4.	John Kennedy	D.	Golf
5.	Abraham Lincoln	E.	Football, golf
6.	Ronald Reagan	F.	Swimming
7.	Gerald Ford	G.	Walking
8.	Jimmy Carter	H.	Football
9.	Harry Truman	I.	Sailing
10.	Richard Nixon	J.	Horseback riding

Alphabet Soup

1. What two major-league baseball players share a first name that contains all five vowels of the alphabet?
2. A palindrome is a word, phrase, or sentence that reads the same backward and forward, like the name Otto or the phrase "Madam, I'm Adam." What major-league ballplayer's last name is a palindrome?

3. There was a basketball player in the 1950s who led the nation in scoring while playing for the Temple University Owls. His last name was spelled without an a, e, i, o, or u, so he was called "the Owl without a vowel." Name him.

The Hollywood Connection

Match the stars on the left with the colleges they attended and the sports they played on the right.

1.	Burt Reynolds	A.	St. Lawrence, wrestling
2.	Jim Brown	B.	Penn, track
3.	Bruce Dern	C.	Syracuse, football, lacrosse
4.	Mike Connors	D.	Florida State, football
5.	Chuck Connors	E.	UCLA, basketball
6.	Kirk Douglas	F.	Seton Hall, basketball, baseball

Touring the Majors

1. Of the four major spectator sports—football, baseball, basketball, and hockey—only three major-league teams don't have nicknames ending with "s." Which are they?
2. The nicknames of the 98 major professional teams in these four sports run almost from A to Z, but not quite. What two letters are not used as the first letter of either a franchise name or a nickname?
3. What two teams have numbers for nicknames?
4. Nine different teams have a color in their names. Which ones are they?
5. Eight teams have nicknames connected with the sea. Name them.
6. Six teams have names referring to geographic areas or features. Which are they?

Doubled Up

Some famous athletes excelled in more than one sport. Match the players on the left, identified with the sport in which they were best known, with their "other" sport on the right.

1.	Bob Gibson, baseball	A.	Basketball, Detroit Pistons
2.	Bob Hayes, football	B.	Basketball, Rochester Royals
3.	Otto Graham, football	C.	Baseball, New York Yankees
4.	Dave DeBusschere, basketball	D.	Volleyball, several teams
5.	George Halas, football	E.	Basketball, Harlem Globetrotters
6.	Ron Reed, baseball	F.	Football, New York, Pittsburgh
7.	Jim Thorpe, football	G.	Track and field, U.S. Olympic team
8.	Wilt Chamberlain, basketball	H.	Baseball, Chicago White Sox
9.	Christy Mathewson, baseball	I.	Baseball, several teams

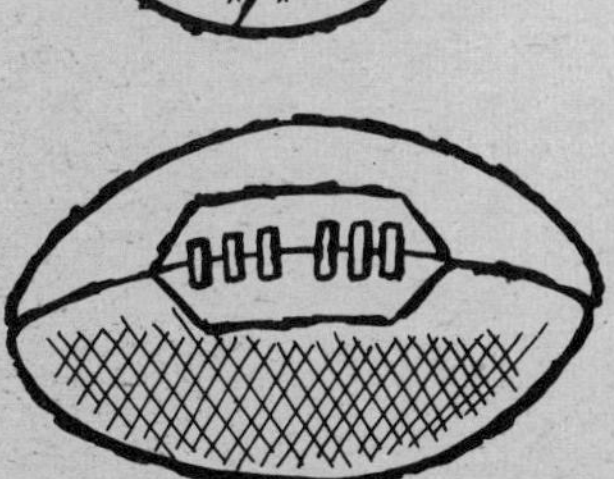

To the Victor . . .

Match the trophy on the left with its receiver on the right.

1. Outland Trophy
2. Sullivan Award
3. Podoloff Cup
4. Naismith Trophy
5. MacArthur Bowl
6. Cy Young Award
7. Art Ross Trophy

A. Best pitcher in each baseball major league
B. The number 1 team in college football
C. Outstanding college lineman
D. Top scorer in the National League
E. Most valuable player in the National Basketball Association
F. Best amateur athlete in the United States
G. Outstanding college basketball player of the year

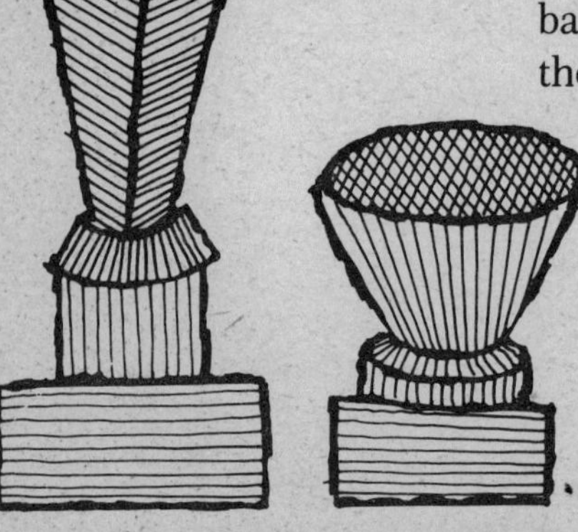

A Silly Billy

Many colleges have mascots. Whose mascot is this?

SPORTS PHOTO SOURCE

Colorful Colleges

College sports are filled with color and excitement. Match the schools on the left with their colorful team nicknames on the right.

1.	Syracuse	A.	Blue Demons
2.	Tulane	B.	Blue Devils
3.	Alabama	C.	Blue Hens
4.	Duke	D.	Redmen
5.	Texas Tech	E.	Big Red
6.	Mississippi State	F.	Red Raiders
7.	Rutgers	G.	Cardinals
8.	Hawaii	H.	Scarlet Knights
9.	Delaware	I.	Crimson Tide
10.	Dartmouth	J.	Golden Eagles
11.	Cornell	K.	Yellow Jackets
12.	Stanford	L.	Orangemen
13.	Tennessee Tech	M.	Big Green
14.	St. John's (N.Y.)	N.	Green Wave
15.	DePaul	O.	Purple Aces
16.	Evansville	P.	Rainbows
17.	Georgia Tech	Q.	Maroons

Cupful

Match the trophies on the left with the sports in which they are awarded on the right.

1. Davis Cup
2. Stanley Cup
3. Colonial Cup
4. America's Cup
5. Ryder Cup
6. Curtis Cup
7. Walker Cup
8. Wightman Cup
9. Grey Cup
10. Little Brown Jug

A. Thoroughbred horse racing
B. Men's professional golf
C. Men's amateur golf
D. Canadian football
E. Harness racing
F. Hockey
G. Yachting
H. Women's amateur golf
I. Women's tennis
J. Men's tennis

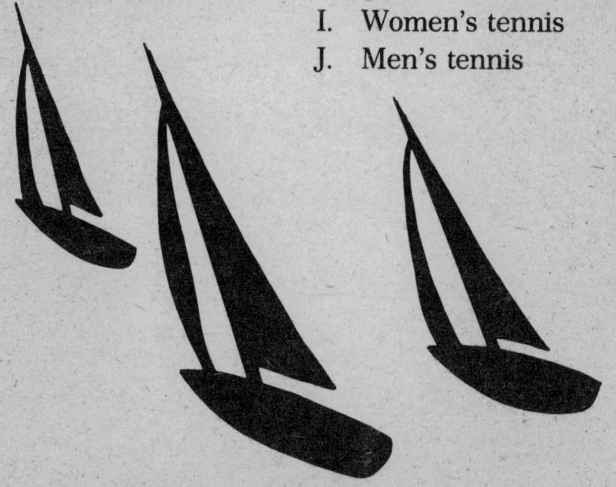

Answers

Balls and Strikes: Baseball

Page 2, Scrambled Big Leaguers

1. Jim Rice, 2. Mike Schmidt, 3. Bob Horner, 4. Cecil Cooper, 5. Richie Zisk, 6. Gary Matthews, 7. Steve Garvey, 8. J. R. Richard, 9. Goose Gossage

Page 2, Easy as Pie

Tom Seaver

Page 4, To Tell the Truth

1. *True*
2. *False*. Aaron finished his career with the Milwaukee Brewers and hit 22 home runs in 1975 and 1976 in the American League.
3. *True*. Bill Terry led the National League with a .401 average and Hack Wilson drove in 190 runs in 1930.
4. *True*. Alou, playing with the Pittsburgh Pirates, won the batting title with a .342 average in 1966, then followed it with a .338 (Roberto Clemente led the league with .357), .332 (Pete Rose batted .335), and .331 (Rose won again with .348).
5. *True*. The MVP award was set up in 1931 when Ruth was near the end of his career.
6. *False*. Thirteen men did it—and Honus Wagner and Max Cary each did it twice.
7. *True*. Although two players—Eddie Morgan of the St. Louis Cardinals, on April 14, 1936, and Chuck Tanner of the Milwaukee Braves, on April 12, 1955—hit home runs on the first pitch thrown to them on opening day, nobody is on record as having hit a home run on the first pitch of the first game of any major-league season.
8. *False*. The poem by Ernest Thayer was first published June 3, 1888, by the San Francisco *Chronicle*, two years before Stengel was born, and 24 years before he started in the majors. The poem is well known because a young comedian named De Wolf Hopper used it in his act.

9. *True.* Rabbit Maranville set the major-league record by coming to bat 672 times in one season without hitting a home run.
10. *False.* The New York Yankees' Bobby Richardson was the Series MVP in 1960 even though Bill Mazeroski's home run gave the Pittsburgh Pirates a dramatic seventh-game victory.
11. *False.* Ruth hit his last three home runs—numbers 712, 713, and 714—on May 25, 1935, while playing with the Boston Braves in the National League. He retired a few days and a couple of games later.
12. *False.* Dave Johnson hit 43 home runs in 1973, yet drove in only 99 runs.
13. *True.* Two came close. In 1913 Walter Johnson won 36 games while giving up 38 walks, and in 1904 Cy Young won 26 games while yielding 28 bases on balls.

Page 6, School for Thought

1-H, 2-E, 3-F, 4-C, 5-D, 6-L, 7-I, 8-G,
9-J, 10-A, 11-B, 12-K

Page 7, Good Morning, America

David Hartman. As host of tv show *Good Morning, America,* he works out with the teams and does interviews.

Page 8, Rain Game

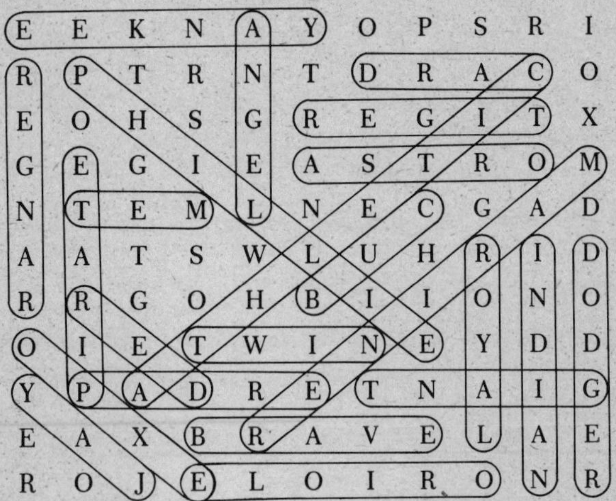

Page 9, Mud Pies

Blackburne discovered that mud found near Willingboro, New Jersey, was just the right thing to take the shine off a baseball without roughing it up. A shiny ball could distract a batter on a sunny day. For years major-league umpires have used the goo, which they refer to as "Lena Blackburne mud."

Page 10, Home-Run Kings

1. Ruth, 60 in 1927; Maris, 61 in 1961
2. Mantle, 52 in 1956, 54 in 1961
3. Aaron, 755; Ruth, 714
4. Mays, 660
5. Mize, 51 in 1947; Maris, 61 in 1961; Ruth, 54 in 1920, 59 in 1921, 60 in 1927, 54 in 1928
6. Mize
7. Gehrig
8. Ruth, in 1926 and 1928

9. Mantle
10. Aaron
11. Robinson
12. Mays
13. Gehrig
14. Ruth, in 1927

Page 12, All in the Family

1-D-e, 2-E-a, 3-A-b, 4-B-c, 5-C-d

Page 12, Color Guide

The Oakland A's are the only major-league team that has green as one of their official colors. The San Diego Padres are the only team with brown, a shade that is officially called Padre Brown, after the color of the robes of the missionaries who settled in California and built Mission San Diego 400 years ago.

Page 13, A Comedy Team

"Who's on First?"

Page 14, The Name Game

1-D, 2-A, 3-B, 4-E, 5-F, 6-C

Page 15, On the Platter

1-D, 2-E, 3-F, 4-C, 5-G, 6-L, 7-A, 8-J,
9-K, 10-M, 11-I, 12-H, 13-B

Page 18, Between the Bases

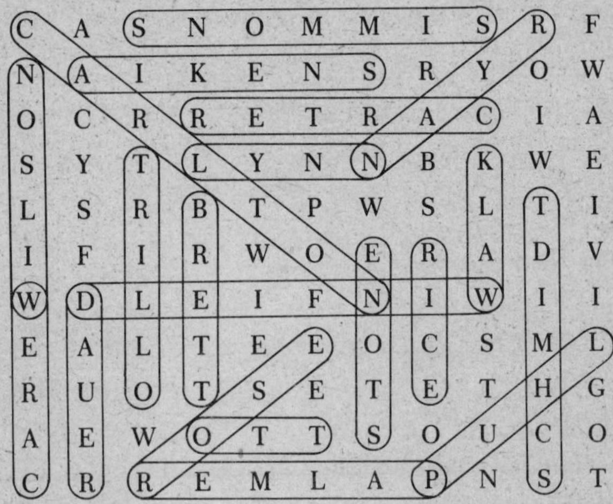

Page 19, Bursting the Bubble

George Brett

Page 20, Completing the Play

1. "ain't."
2. "you're out of it."
3. "no hit."
4. "play this game?"
5. "nothin'."

Page 21, Unlisted Number

He didn't wear a number. Major-league clubs didn't start putting numbers on uniforms until the 1930s.

Page 22, Home, Sweet Home

1-M-a, 2-P-q, 3-J-k, 4-G-x, 5-N-c, 6-A-n, 7-Q-t, 8-R-g, 9-K-m, 10-B-o, 11-S-v, 12-D-i, 13-T-w, 14-V-p, 15-C-d, 16-W-u, 17-F-r, 18-X-s, 19-O-b, 20-Y-h, 21-Z-f, 22-L-l, 23-I-j, 24-E-e, 25-U-g, 26-H-p

Page 24, Another Sport

They were all quarterbacks on their college football teams.

Page 24, The Rifleman

Chuck Connors

Page 25, Perfection

1. Len Barker
2. Babe Ruth, in the days before he became a right fielder and home-run hitter, pitched for the Boston Red Sox. In this game, Ruth was the starting pitcher. He walked the first batter—and started an argument with the umpire that caused Ruth to be thrown out of the game. Ernie Shore came in to pitch. The base runner was caught trying to steal, and Shore retired the next 26 batters in order, so he was credited with a perfect game.
3. Larsen, pitching for the New York Yankees, blanked Sal Maglie and the Brooklyn Dodgers, 2–0.
4. 97
5. The Cubs' Bob Hendley, Koufax's opponent, narrowly missed pitching his own perfect game, giving up a walk in the fifth inning and then losing the no-hitter on a double in the seventh. In both cases it was Lou Johnson who got on base. The second time Johnson was on, he managed to move around the bases without another hit by his teammates, and then scored on an error. The two teams, with one hit between them, established a major-league record for fewest hits in a game by two teams.

Page 26, Quick Change

The two players were traded for each other between games of the morning/afternoon doubleheader.

Page 27, Crosstown Rivalries

1-G, J; 2-C, I; 3-A, H; 4-B, F; 5-D, E

Page 27, Mound Magic

When Altrock came into the game in the ninth inning, the bases were full and two men were out. Before Altrock threw his first pitch, he picked a runner off base. Chicago then went on to win the game in the bottom half of the inning.

Page 28, Mystery Ms.

Babe Didrikson. She never pitched in an official game, but Babe took the mound in several exhibition contests, including one for the Brooklyn Dodgers against the Philadelphia A's.

Page 29, A Rare Byrd

Playing with the New York Yankees from 1929 to 1934, Byrd often pinch-ran for Ruth or otherwise replaced him for defensive purposes late in a game.

Page 29, An Old Oriole

c

Page 29, Triple Threat

36

Page 30, Old-Timers

Jim Kaat, who started his career with the Washington Senators; Tim McCarver, who began with the St. Louis Cardinals; and Willie McCovey, who broke in with the San Francisco Giants. All started playing in 1959. Overall, there have been 17 players whose major-league careers have spanned four decades.

Minnie Minoso

Page 30, Peanuts, Popcorn

Former President Jimmy Carter

Page 32, Baseball Boggling

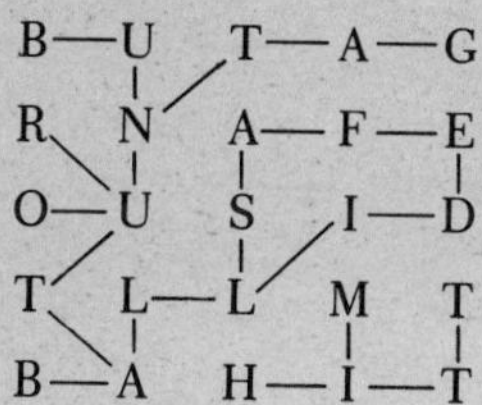

Kickoff: Football

Page 34, Scrambled Quarterbacks

1. Danny White, 2. Brian Sipe, 3. Bert Jones, 4. Dan Fouts, 5. Ron Jaworski, 6. Jim Zorn, 7. Vince Evans, 8. Joe Theisman, 9. Steve Grogan, 10. Steve Bartkowski

Page 34, Handsome Hero

Burt Reynolds

Page 36; Lights, Camera, Action . . .

1-E, 2-F, 3-A, 4-D, 5-G, 6-C, 7-B

Page 36, Alias

1. Sonny, 2. Buck, 3. Deacon, 4. Bubba, 5. Bart, 6. Coy, 7. Rocky, 8. Mean Joe, 9. D.D., 10. White Shoes, 11. Archie

Page 37, Wrong-Way Runs

Jim Marshall was the defensive end for the Vikings whose name is uttered in the same breath as Riegels'. It was on October 25, 1964, in a game against the San Francisco 49ers at Kezar Stadium that Marshall, an All-Star during his prime, made his famous wrong-way run. At least Marshall had some of his embarrassment erased when the Vikings finally won the game, 27–22, in spite of his contribution to the 49ers' total.

Page 39, Varsity Show

1-E, 2-G, 3-D, 4-I, 5-C, 6-J, 7-B, 8-H, 9-A, 10-F

Page 40, In the Huddle

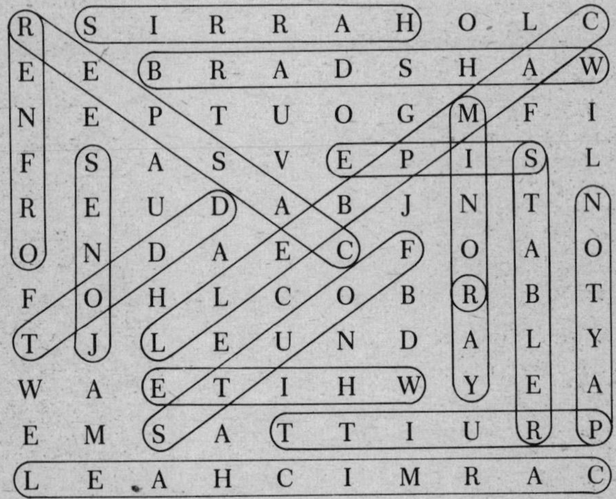

Page 41, Calling the Signals

John Fitzgerald Kennedy

Page 42, Just for Kicks

b

Page 42, A Catch to It

1. Harold Carmichael, 127; and Mel Gray, 105
2. With 22 seconds left in the game, Pittsburgh was trailing the Oakland Raiders, 7–6. The Steelers had the ball on the fourth down with 10 yards to go for a first down on their own 40-yard line. Quarterback Terry Bradshaw threw a pass to running back John (Frenchy) Fuqua. Oakland defender Jack Tatum —and this point has always been disputed by Tatum, the Oakland Raiders, and their fans—deflected the ball, which bounced high in the air. Harris ran under the ball, caught it, and headed for the end zone and a touchdown. Pittsburgh won the game, 13–7.
3. Howard was on the Dallas team that lost to Pittsburgh in Super Bowl X, but he did score on a 34-yard pass during the game. Not only was that Howard's first catch as a pro, but he became the first rookie to have a TD reception in the Super Bowl. Howard was injured in an exhibition before the next season began and never again played in the NFL. He is the only player whose only NFL pass reception was a TD catch in the Super Bowl.

Page 43, Quick Draw

American Football League

Page 43, Teasers

1. *True*, 2. *False* (1973, 1974), 3. *True*, 4. *True*, 5. *False* (Oakland, 1981), 6. *False*, 7. *False* (they've won 7), 8. *False* (Pittsburgh has won 4), 9. *True*

Page 44, Fast on His Feet

Jimmy Brown

Page 45, Undefeated, Untied, and . . .

Plainfield Teachers College did not exist. The school, the team, and Johnny Chung lived only in the active imaginations of a group of New York stockbrokers. The chief ringleader was Morris Newburger, a 35-year-old fan. Newburger and his group would call the newspapers on Saturday to report the scores and story of the game, just as if there really were a Plainfield College. Each week the story had to get a little better, so Plainfield kept winning, the papers were told, and Chung kept scoring. There were even details of how Chung ate rice between halves. As the legend grew some reporters from the newspapers tried to track down Plainfield Teachers College and Johnny Chung, and the whole hoax was revealed. But for most of one season, the college was as good as any team that *never* played.

Page 46, Locate the Bowl

1-P, 2-N, 3-D, 4-I, 5-K, 6-J, 7-L,
8-O, 9-H, 10-A, 11-E, 12-G, 13-B, 14-C,
15-F, 16-M

Page 47, Punt Parade

d

Page 48, Justice Prevails

Byron (Whizzer) White

Page 50, A Tale of Suspense

Alabama fullback Tommy Lewis was on the sideline when he saw Moegle coming down the field with no one near him. Lewis illegally dashed onto the field and tackled Moegle. Just as quickly, he ran back to the bench. Referee Cliff Shaw was stunned, as was everyone else, but then he raised his arms into the air, signaling a touchdown for Moegle and Rice. Shaw later explained that though he had never seen anything like it before, he figured Moegle would have made it all the way to the end zone and should be awarded the touchdown. The score put Rice up, 14–6, at halftime, and the Owls went on to a 28–6 victory without any more interference from the Alabama bench.

Page 51, Flying High

The U.S. Air Force Academy. They flew 24,372 miles, which is just about equal to one trip around the world.

Page 51, Cumberland's Gap

Back in 1916, Cumberland fielded a team after receiving a guarantee of $500 from Georgia Tech to play a game. That was a lot of money in those days, and would go far in buying equipment for the small school's sports program. The fact that Georgia Tech was big, strong, and one of the best teams in the country didn't scare Cumberland. Even if Cumberland lost, it would be for a good cause. As soon as the game started, though, the Cumberland team knew something was wrong. Tech rolled up 63 points in the first quarter. The Ramblin' Wreck didn't stop there. Tech kept right on scoring points, 222 of them to be exact, and little Cumberland didn't get near the goal line all day. But the 222–0 verdict did get Cumberland into the record book as being on the wrong side of the most one-sided game in history.

Page 52, Galloping Backfield

c

Page 53, On the Line

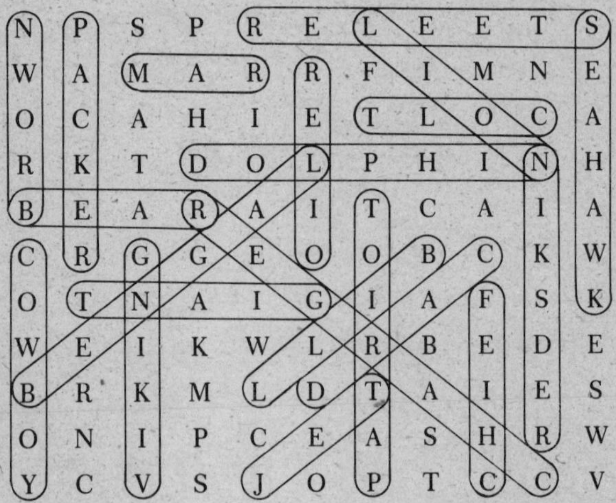

Page 54, Hip, Hip, Hooray

1-E, 2-F, 3-D, 4-C, 5-B, 6-A

Page 54, Game Breakers

1. d; 2. a; 3. c; 4. d, on six touchdowns and seven points after touchdowns; 5. b, 65 and 64 yards against Baylor, October 16, 1976

Page 57, Breaking In with a Bang

a, b, e, f, h

Page 57, Surprise Ending

Officials of the National Broadcasting Company, which televised the game, decided to pass up the final seconds of the contest. Since it had run longer than the three hours the network had allotted for it, the NBC people went ahead with the regularly scheduled program, a tv version of *Heidi*.

Thousands of calls poured into the NBC switchboard and to affiliates around the country. Even the police emergency number in New York City was tied up by hometown fans who wanted to see their Jets do battle with the Raiders.

They probably wouldn't have been very happy, though, if they *had* seen the game's end—because what they missed was a touchdown by Oakland and, on the next kickoff, a fumble by the Jets that led to another touchdown by the Raiders. This made Oakland the winner, 43–32. All that action happened during the last minute.

The game came to be known as "The Heidi Game" and will forever be an embarrassment to NBC. (The Jets did better later that year, going on to win the AFL championship and to become the first AFL team to win a Super Bowl.)

Page 58, One for the Gipper

Ronald Reagan, President of the United States

Page 60, Football Boggling

```
B     K    A—T     R
|     |  /    /    |
A—C       C—H     U
                  /
L—O       E—N     G
   |       /     /
P     S    D    A—I
|     |    |       |
A—S       O—W—N
```

The Backboard Jumble: Basketball

Page 62, Scrambled Dribblers

1. Alvan Adams, 2. Cedric Maxwell, 3. Julius Erving, 4. Marques Johnson, 5. Swen Nater, 6. Kareem Abdul-Jabbar, 7. George Gervin, 8. Adrian Dantley, 9. David Thompson, 10. Michael Ray Richardson

Page 62, Bridging Leagues

Julius (Dr. J) Erving

Page 64, The NBA Game

First Quarter
1. d, 2. c, 3. d, 4. a, 5. *False,* 6. d, 7. *True,* 8. c, 9. a, 10. b, 11. d, 12. c

Second Quarter
1-K, 2-I, 3-G, 4-L, 5-E, 6-H, 7-D, 8-C, 9-A, 10-J, 11-F, 12-B
Three-Pointer: Hershey, Pennsylvania

Third Quarter
1. a, 2. c, 3. b, 4. *True,* 5. *True,* 6. c, 7. d, 8. a, 9. d, 10. *True,* 11. *False,* 12. c, 13. a, 14. *True,* 15. *False,* 16. *False*

Fourth Quarter
1. a-D, b-G, c-A, d-C, e-F, f-H, g-E, h-B; 2. b; 3. *False*; 4. *True*; 5. c; 6. b; 7. d; 8. b (172 games); 9. a-D, b-C, c-E, d-B, e-A, f-G, g-F

Page 70, Woody Dribbles

The New York Knickerbockers. Woody Allen got a chance to play with some other actors and a few of the Knicks at Madison Square Garden during the filming of *Annie Hall.*

Page 71, Around the Hoop

1. b, c, d, e, g, h, j
2. b, c, d, g, i, j
3. b, c, e, h
4. a, d, e, f, g, i, j

5. *True.* Leroy Wright, Pacific, 1959–60; Jerry Lucas, Ohio State, 1961–62; Artis Gilmore, Jacksonville, 1970–71; and Kermit Washington, American, 1972–73, did it for only two years in a row.

Page 73, Name Tags

1-C, 2-E, 3-D, 4-B, 5-A

Page 74, High-School Wonders

1-C, 2-E, 3-A, 4-F, 5-D, 6-B

Page 74, Pivot Play

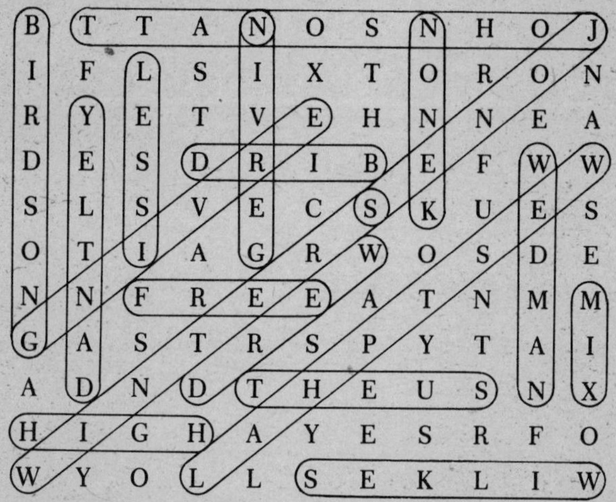

Page 76, A Fitting Label

1-C, 2-E, 3-A, 4-G, 5-H, 6-B, 7-F, 8-D

Page 76, The Other League

1-N, 2-L, 3-G, 4-O, 5-C, 6-E, 7-I, 8-J, 9-F, 10-H, 11-A, 12-D, 13-K, 14-B, 15-M

Page 78, Hidden Hoopsters

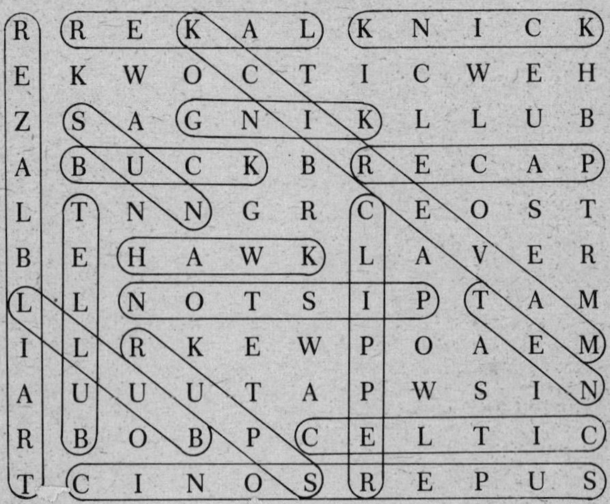

Page 79, A Slamdunk in Hollywood

Bill Cosby

Page 80, Basketball Boggling

```
R\  M   J   N—E
  \             |
P  >I   O   S   T
|  /        |   |
M<  J   G\  H—O
  \ |     \   /
O—U  /A—O—K
|   | /         |
F   L/  D—U—N
```

Faceoff: Ice Hockey

Page 82, Scrambled Icemen

1. Bobby Clarke, 2. Larry Robinson, 3. Marc Tardif, 4. Mike Bossy, 5. Ron Duguay, 6. Charlie Simmer, 7. Wayne Gretzky, 8. Mike Liut, 9. Darryl Sittler, 10. Wayne Babych

Page 82, Leading Man

Paul Newman

Page 84, Think Rink

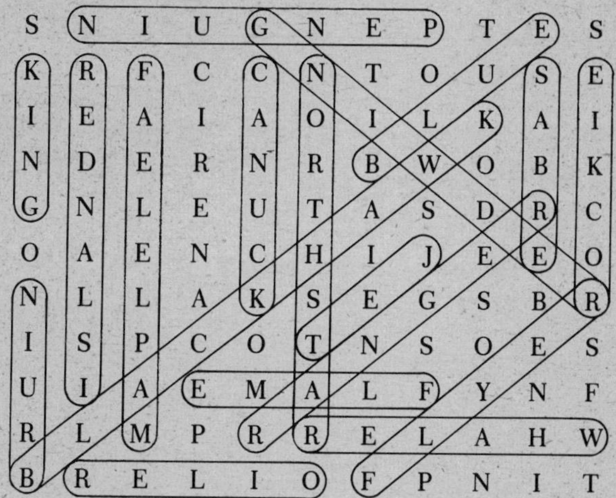

Page 86, On the Line

1-E, 2-G, 3-A, 4-B, 5-I, 6-H, 7-C, 8-F, 9-D

Page 87, Holiday on Ice?

False. On February 20, 1944, the Chicago Black Hawks and the Toronto Maple Leafs skated to an 0–0 tie in a game that took only 1 hour and 55 minutes to play because no penalties were called on either team.

Page 87, Disappearing Act

1-D, 2-C, 3-A, 4-B

Page 88, Puck Soup

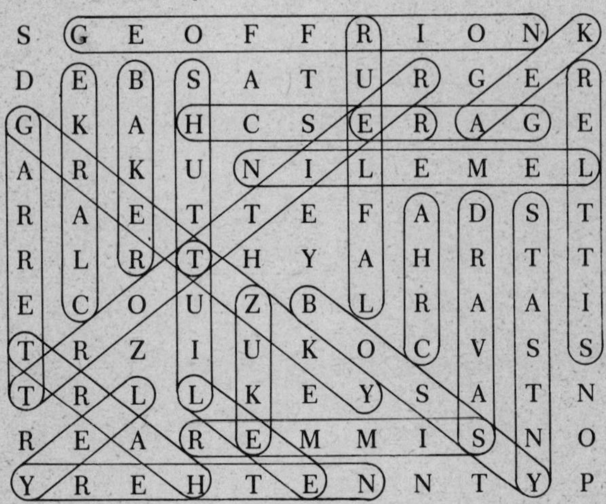

Page 89, Another Part of the Ice

1-C, 2-E, 3-G, 4-F, 5-A, 6-D, 7-B

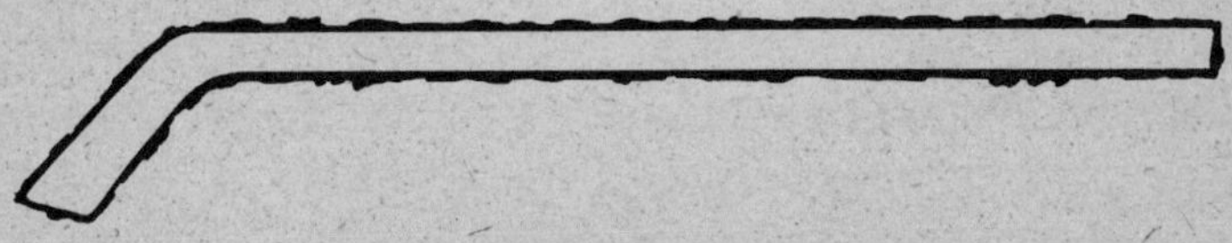

Page 90, Hockey Boggling

```
S—A   S—T—I
|  |  | / /
H  V—E—C—K
|     |     |
O  L  N  U—C
|  |       \
T  A  K—A  P
   |  |  |
G—O  S  T—E
```

Of Lobs and Links: Tennis and Golf

Page 92, Loving Cup

c, f, g, i, k, l

Page 92, Court Jester

French. Jimmy Connors was banned by the French from competing in the event after he signed a contract to play in the new World Team Tennis League in the U.S., which the Europeans considered a threat to their major summer tournaments.

Page 94, A Mixed Volley

1. a, Billie Jean King won 20; 2. d; 3. 63; 4. b

Page 95, Have Racket, Will Travel

1-I, 2-D, 3-H, 4-C, 5-J, 6-A, 7-M, 8-L, 9-F, 10-B, 11-G, 12-E, 13-K

Page 97, Battle of the Sexes

Billie Jean King

Page 98, Chip Shots

1. d, 2. a, 3. d

Page 99, Prize Money

1. a; 2. c; 3. d; 4. c; 5. Kathy Whitworth, who earned $1,008,469 during her 23-year professional career

Page 100, Iron Arm

82

In the Ring: Boxing

Page 102, A Comic Twist

Bob Hope. Before he became an entertainer, Hope fought in the Cleveland area under the name of Packy East. Since he became a comedian, Hope has been staging exhibitions against champion fighters for more than 40 years.

Page 102, Film Fighters

1-D, 2-E, 3-A, 4-F, 5-C, 6-B

Page 103, Ring King

1. 25; 2. 2 minutes, 4 seconds of the first round; 3. "can't hide"; 4. Bomber; 5. d; 6. 54 knockouts, 5 of which were in the first round

Page 105, Boxing Hopeful

Jack Dempsey

Page 106, Sultan of Swat

Babe Ruth

Page 107, Sweet Champion

Sugar Ray Robinson

Page 107, Punching Bag

d

Page 108, Clean Slate

b. Marciano retired unbeaten after winning 49 professional fights, 43 by knockout and 6 by decision.

The Olympic Game

Page 110, Feats of Gold

a, b, k, l

Page 110, Unparalleled

Romania's Nadia Comaneci, the 14-year-old who won seven 10s (the highest score possible) on the way to three gold medals in the 1976 Olympic Games

Page 112, Doubles

1-D, 2-F, 3-A, 4-E, 5-B, 6-C

Page 112, Leaps and Bounds

b. The earlier record of 27 feet, 4 ¾ inches was shared by Ralph Boston of the U.S. and Igor Ter-Ovanesyan of the U.S.S.R.

Page 113, Roll Out the Barrel

False

Page 114, Olympic Carnival

1. b; 2. a, d; 3. *False*. The Americans had won in an equally spectacular upset in 1960 in Squaw Valley, California; 4. a, d, e (b, flush, is used in downhill skiing; c, icing, is a hockey term; f, pasgang, is used in cross-country skiing)

Page 114, Icy Victory

b

Page 116, On the Button

Figure skating

Page 116, A Winning Figure

c

Page 118, Fadeouts

b, c, d, g, h

On Horseback

Page 120, Winning the West

A former stagecoach driver named Joe Berry finished first, after 13 days and 16 hours. But since Berry had helped lay out the route, he was declared ineligible. Emmett Albright finished 1 hour and 45 minutes later, but he, too, was disqualified after it was learned that he had shipped himself and his horse 100 miles in a railroad boxcar. Joe Gillespie, the heaviest rider at 185 pounds, was declared the winner, taking 13 days and 20 hours. Second, in the official standings, was Charles Smith, who finished 17 minutes behind Gillespie.

Page 120, Royal Rider

Prince Charles of England, whose marriage to Lady Diana was a royal event.

Page 122, On the Right Track

1-C, 2-E, 3-A, 4-F, 5-D, 6-B

Page 122, Of Phillies and Fillies

True. A filly named Genuine Risk won the 1980 Kentucky Derby, and the Phillies won the 1980 World Series.

Page 123, The Lady in Silks

c

Page 124, Run for the Roses

Shoemaker, who has ridden more winning horses than any other jockey in history, had misjudged the finish line. Gallant Man hadn't yet crossed it. After Shoemaker stood up on the horse, he realized his mistake and plopped back down in the saddle. It was too late, and Gallant Man was beaten by a narrow margin.

A Mixed Bag

Page 126, Brains + Brawn

1-D, 2-E, 3-B and D, 4-A, 5-C

Page 127, Vaulting to the Moon

Buzz Aldrin

Page 128, A Striking Game

1. 27, 2. 33, 3. 19

Page 128, Solo Sailor

d

Page 129, Kicking It Around

E K A U Q H T R A E K

R D I P L O M A T B C

E P A C E T I H W L E

M R W O E R G S M I N

O E D A C E T Z A Z H

O T M O H L Z B W Z G

B E S T I L R G S A U

N M T M E I D W O R O

O C I S F R U S O D R

I O N R E D N U O S S

S S G S T R I K E R T

Page 130, A Battering Ram

Merlin Olsen

Page 131, By the Numbers

1-D, 2-F, 3-C, 4-H, 5-J, 6-G, 7-I, 8-B, 9-E, 10-A

Page 131, Marathon Swim

7 hours, 57 minutes

Page 132, Home on the Range

Gene Autry

Page 133, Streaking

1. a, 2. d, 3. b, 4. c, 5. a

Page 134, Sporting Couples

1-E, 2-A, 3-B, 4-C, 5-D

Page 135, Family Sports

1-D, 2-A, 3-F, 4-B, 5-C, 6-E

Page 135, The Most Popular Run

The 90 feet between bases on a baseball diamond

Page 136, Medical Report

1. His nose
2. Ryder, a victim of polio, was on crutches—and wanted to prove he could do it.
3. Pete Gray had only one arm. He batted one-handed. When he was in the field, he caught the ball in his one hand, flipped it into the air, stuck the glove under the stump of his other arm, caught the ball, and made his throw.
4. "Three-Finger" Brown

Page 137, Name Change

1-B, 2-C, 3-D, 4-A

Page 137, A Touch of Sport

b, was a radio sportscaster; d, was a sportswriter in New York just before his death; g, was a sportswriter before turning to fiction.

Page 138, Of Skates and Scalpels

Tenley Albright

Page 139, The Flush of Youth

1. Thirteen years, 9 months
2. Fifteen years, 10 months
3. Brown, who hit his homer off Pittsburgh's Preacher Roe, was 17 years old at the time.
4. Fifteen years, 10 months. Dod also won the Wimbledon title in 1888, 1891, 1892, and 1893.
5. Paciorek underwent back surgery before the 1964 season. He tried playing again in the minor leagues, but retired from baseball in 1968 without ever making it back to the major leagues.
6. Eight

Page 141, Brotherly Love

1-D, 2-G, 3-J, 4-H, 5-A, 6-C, 7-F, 8-B, 9-E, 10-I

Page 142, Fast on the Trigger

Johnny Bench

Page 143, The Movie Game

1-C, 2-F, 3-D, 4-A, 5-G, 6-E, 7-J 8-I, 9-K, 10-L, 11-B, 12-H

Page 144, Going Up

1,575

Page 145, Speaking of Sports

1-C, 2-F, 3-H, 4-A, 5-I, 6-E and G, 7-B, 8-D and C, 9-G

Page 145, Presidents in Sport

1-F, 2-D, 3-A, 4-I, 5-B, 6-J, 7-E, 8-C, 9-G, 10-H

Page 146, Alphabet Soup

1. Aurelio Rodriguez, Aurelio Lopez; 2. Toby Harrah; 3. Bill Mlkvy

Page 147, The Hollywood Connection

1-D, 2-C, 3-B, 4-E, 5-F, 6-A

Page 148, Touring the Majors

1. Utah Jazz, Boston Red Sox, Chicago White Sox
2. X and Z
3. San Francisco 49ers, Philadelphia 76ers
4. Boston Red Sox, Toronto Blue Jays, Chicago White Sox, Cincinnati Reds, Cleveland Browns, Washington Redskins, Detroit Red Wings, St. Louis Blues, and Chicago Black Hawks
5. Seattle Mariners, Pittsburgh Pirates, Miami Dolphins, Seattle Seahawks, Hartford Whalers, Minnesota Vikings, Tampa Bay Buccaneers, San Diego Clippers
6. Minnesota North Stars, Quebec Nordiques, Montreal Canadiens, Colorado Rockies, New York Islanders, Los Angeles Lakers

Page 148, Doubled Up

1-E, 2-G, 3-B, 4-H, 5-C, 6-A, 7-I and G, 8-D, 9-F

Page 150, To the Victor . . .

1-C, 2-F, 3-E, 4-G, 5-B, 6-A, 7-D

Page 151, A Silly Billy

Navy (U.S. Naval Academy)

Page 152, Colorful Colleges

1-L, 2-N, 3-I, 4-B, 5-F, 6-Q, 7-H, 8-P,
9-C, 10-M, 11-E, 12-G, 13-J, 14-D, 15-A, 16-O,
17-K

Page 153, Cupful

1-J, 2-F, 3-A, 4-G, 5-B, 6-H, 7-C, 8-I,
9-D, 10-E